Lossie:
Live to Laugh

Lois Sexton Smith

Introduction by Annette Smith Stilwell

Stilwell, Buda, Burch, LLC
Atlanta
2019

Introduction

Mama was a storyteller. She loved stories. She loved people, most especially she loved to laugh. Long before the internet, laughter was her invisible link to everyone around her. Her real name was Lois Lynnette Sexton Smith but everyone called her "Lossie".

She was a paraplegic.

Mama's story is not about overcoming limitations but about an amazing woman who overcame barriers against all odds. The is a window into the life of a woman who recognized only her strengths, and ran her life accordingly.

I was the fortunate middle child of an exceptional woman. She and her mother taught me the truly important things in life—love of family, truth, light, happiness and a keen interest in all that was going on around her. To grow up in the presence of such positive, down-to-earth, but fun people gave me a true sense of self. I never considered that my Mama was handicapped.

She drove me places, she wrote the news, she knew everybody. I remember when she got her first Apple computer she would sit for hours at her desk, with me reading in a chair behind her, wondering whether she would ever stop typing and talk to me.

She had a dark room and developed her own pictures. When the red light was on, we couldn't open the door. I remember also waiting outside that door.

Mama started this book in 1974. She typed it with an electric typewriter. She worked and worked on it throughout my childhood. When I graduated from college and had access to a copy machine, I made copies for her. I kept a copy with hopes of helping her get it published.

For many years, I would pick it up from time to time but I never got past just reading. Many years later I realized that I could scan the pages and then share the pages. This began a communal project for my family. You will read about some of the relatives that played an important role in this story. Sam (my brother and Lossie's first born) and Veronica Smith. Bobby (son of Lois's sister Beatrice) and Ann Howard, Laura Howard (son of Bea's son Tommy) and Gwyn Newsom (daughter of Cousin Marie). I recruited them to spend long weekends of sitting around a dining room table, computers at hand, going page-by-page over Mama's writing.

We did not change Mama's words, just the typos and formatting. It has given us many special times of laughter and tears as we worked together.

What Mama started, we hoped to finish, with the same spirit, joy, inspiration and fun that she felt. This, indeed, has been a true labor of love. I have a feeling Lossie is smiling and laughing.

—Annette Smith Stillwell

Lois and Bill

1

Chapter One

In my lifetime having laughter to overcome my tears, the first time I cried occurred as a doctor gave my bottom a quick slap seconds after I scooted from the restrictiveness of my mother's womb. I should have laughed because an innate feature of my personality made me love both laughter and freedom from the moment I gasped for my first breath of life. The year was 1919. Huey P. Long had entered into politics in my birth state, Louisiana, where oil and gas were emerging industries. These facts were remote from my birth but they quickly touched my life to play a major role in my family's destiny.

My father found his first employment in lumber. After he finished his business studies, he started to work as a bookkeeper for a Louisiana lumber company. During this time romance came his way when my mother, who lived in North Carolina, made a trip to Louisiana to visit one of her brothers who worked for the same company as my father. Samuel Otis Sexton and Annie Laurie Phifer met and soon married on September 11, 1915. After their marriage and after World War I ended, the excessive need for lumber diminished as petroleum products became more in demand. This influenced my daddy to change employment from the lumber industry to an oil refinery company.

Soon after leaving the lumber yards for oil refinery grounds, Sam Sexton became a father for his third time when I was born on August 5, 1919. He also became a land owner. Two months after I was born, he bought his first tract of land, a plot of forty acres. The following month he bought sixty more acres, and before the year ended he became an oil and gas lessor when he leased his land to the Texas Company.

About the same time my father changed employment, Huey Long started his political career by winning a seat on the Louisiana Railroad Commission which regulated controls over the lumber and gas industries. Early in his career as a politician who wanted to impress upon voters that he was a "friend of the people," Long introduced state legislation requiring benefits to be paid to maimed or killed lumber and oil workers and to their widows. This legislation passed.

Two years after my birth, Long's legislation benefited my family when my father was seriously injured at the oil refinery where he worked. A boiler exploded on the morning of March 21, 1922, just as he rode onto the grounds. In a freak accident, my father was the only person injured when he was struck by flying metal. Although critically injured, he was not rendered unconscious but was unable to talk because some of the metal fragments had broken his jaw bones. Coupled with the shock of my father's accident, my mother, overcome with disquieting fear, grabbed us three children to take with her as she rushed to my daddy's side. She became more alarmed when she was told there was no ambulance available in the refinery area of Ruston and that my father had been placed in the baggage room of the train depot, where he lay on a baggage cart to wait for a train to carry him to the hospital in Shreveport.

Mama remembered "some men who worked with your daddy helped me carry you children to the train station," my mother later told us. She added a thing that remained vivid in her memory: "When your Daddy saw us enter the depot, tears started rolling down his face."

At the time Daddy suffered his injuries, my sister Beatrice was five, my brother Thomas was three, and I was two. Filled with grief, my mother took us with her as she boarded the train's baggage car at the same time my father was loaded onto it. As the train swayed and bumped along on its scheduled run to Shreveport, Mama said, "Six men at a time took turns to hold Sam's stretcher so that the movement of the train would not increase his suffering."

She at times recalled for us the memory of how pathetically sad our bereaved family had looked, as we huddled together in the baggage car, in terror over the uncertainty of our plight. Mama also later told us that while we were waiting for the train to arrive, "Your Daddy wanted to talk but he couldn't. Each time he looked at you children, more tears would roll down his cheeks." She added, "He cradled your face in one hand and looked at me with his eyes as if he were trying to ask, 'What will happen to my baby?'"

We never found out what our father wanted to say because he died before he reached the hospital, dying on the same day he was injured. He was only twenty-seven years old.

Through the years, I often heard my mother agonize recalling the last minutes of life for my father. In anguish, she would ask herself, "I wonder what it was that Sam wanted to say?" Knowing he wanted to say something and could not was a hurt my mother carried with her until she died forty-three years later. My mother must have loved my father deeply. She was pretty as a young girl and young looking in her later years. Several men made an effort to court her but she never dated again. We three children became her life.

After my father's death, Mama took us three half orphans to Rodessa, Louisiana, where we lived with my father's daddy, Thomas Fincher Sexton, who was a widower. My daddy was buried a short distance down a sand bed road from the Sexton's homeplace, in a cemetery located on property owned by our family.

My mother occupied herself by settling her business and making arrangements to receive financial benefits from Gulf Oil, the company my father had worked for when he was accidentally killed. Those benefits were the result of Huey P. Long's legislative accomplishment; no matter what historians may say about Long's political career, I will always be thankful for his work benefiting "the people" since our family had become a member of that group.

At the time of my daddy's death, the Texas Company still held oil and gas leases on my father's and the Sexton family land. At times, as I was growing up, my mother and Grandpa Sexton leased our land to different lessees, which kept the hope forever dangling in our thoughts that one day oil would be found on our property.

During the winter of the year my father died, the hopes of oil were not on my mother's mind. Instead, her thoughts were on the survival of her only son, Thomas, who had developed pneumonia. I was too young to realize how seriously ill he was but sister Beatrice was old enough to understand the anxiety my mother and the Sexton family had during his illness.

Recalling the limited medical knowledge of pneumonia at that time, Beatrice said, "I remember how Thomas' high fever stayed a constant threat to his recovery, and how different ones staying at Grandpa's took turns day and night going outside in the cold to bring in ice from the yard to place on Thomas to make his raging fever leave." Prayers and ice packs worked because Thomas lived.

At the onset of his illness, he was too sick to be moved. Grandma Sexton's sister, Lettie Slaughter, had married a doctor, W.B. Lawton. When we were sick, Mama would pack us up and take us to the Lawtons where we stayed with them while Dr. Lawton doctored whichever one of us was sick.

Dr. Lawton had a small office building in the front yard of his residence. On one of our "sick" visits to the Lawtons, we Sexton three amused ourselves by peeping through Dr. Lawton's office windows while he was waiting on his patients. One patient I keenly watched was a female patient who had a pus-filled boil on her bosom. I still have mental pictures of my great uncle lancing that boil, a vivid sight that left me dreading having anything to ever happen to my bosoms.

After the heart-breaking trauma Mama experienced with the death of her husband Sam and Thomas' recovery from pneumonia, "Widow Anne" decided to return to North Carolina where her family held deep roots and still lived on land grant property.

In 1923, with my father's insurance and death benefits in hand, my mother clutched her toddler Lois in her arms as her two walkers pulled at her skirt, and boarded a train to take us back to the state of her birth. Herding her fatherless children over a thousand miles on a day coach took a great deal of courage and spirit for a lady dressed in her new widow's black. The desire to keep her family together and make a new home for her children gave her the strength to spur on. The train ride to North Carolina was as sad for my mother as the one that carried Daddy to Shreveport, only it lasted longer.

Arriving back in Mama's home county, we moved in with Grandma Emma Ramseur Phifer, who had been a widow since Grandpa's death the year I was born. We made our home in Bessemer City, where Grandpa Phifer built the house in 1903 because he thought his twelve children would receive better educations in the town schools than they could in rural schools that operated under such names as Possum Trot, Turkey Run and Hog's Hill. Consequently, my mother was one of the four students, all females, who were Bessemer City's first graded school graduation class.

For several years, the Phifers kept their rural homeplace in addition to their house in town. It turned out that my grandparents could bring their children to town, but "couldn't get the country out of their boys." Whenever the Phifer boys looked out a school window to see a wagon from their farm riding into town, they climbed out the window and jumped onto the wagon to ride it back to the farm. Riding on wagons must have been the only thing that pleased the Phifer boys about the farm because none of them took up farming as their livelihood.

Once she was back with her family, Mama's five brothers and six sisters rallied to help "Annie and her orphans." This amounted to a lot of help because ten of the Phifer's dozen were married with the majority of them living within visiting distance of Bessemer City. Mama's brothers were kind hearted and gentle. So were her sisters. They all had one thing in common: they loved to give advice on everything to everybody. This trait turned out to be an advantage for us Sexton kids. My six aunts, filled with loving concern for Annie's children, strove to outdo one another in the amount of advice they doled out, as well as helping my mother in rearing us.

In later years, I frequently commented, "I don't know what it would be like to have a father, but I do know what it's like to have seven mothers to love me."

Soon after our arrival in Bessemer City, my mother found and bought the house she wanted, and in it we grew up as a tightly knit family. Thanks to her family, friends, and preacher, my mother never lacked for an advisory council. They guided her when to take off my winter underwear, how long to make my dresses, the time to use a keen switch from a peach tree in our yard, and when to administer doses of castor oil, which was the cure-all remedy of my childhood.

Winter underwear became a part of my underclothing when we moved to North Carolina. It kept me comfortably warm when outdoors and uncomfortably warm indoors. Along with fireplaces, coal and wood- burning heaters could throw out the heat. As a rule, one stayed in the front room to stay warm. The only time my mother heated a bedroom was when we had company, and the door to our spare bedroom was left open to let a little heat seep into the room for the comfort of our guests.

Today's kids will never know the ordeal of having to wear

winter underwear for months as I did. How I hated wearing those most essential garments. Even though I won the battle for cotton long Johns over woolen ones, I still resented their whiteness sticking out from under my dress sleeves, and their bulkiness that made my legs look fat with them tucked inside my brown cotton stockings. Early signs of spring were always welcomed occurrences.

How delightful the naked feeling was on the first warm day that signaled it was time to take off winter underwear and roll down long cotton stockings. I can still remember the pleasant sensation I had the first moments when the hem of my skirt first brushed against my naked thighs.

Wearing that dreaded under garment made me conscious of a rhyme my Uncle John Doyle taught me while I was growing up: "Bought a suit of underwear the other day to keep the cold and air away. Wore it three years without exaggeration. Couldn't get it off because I lost the combination." How I prayed I would never lose the combination!

In grammar grades I must have worn my dresses to the high water mark. I can still feel the critical eyes my Grandmother Phifer would cast upon my brief skirts. She would flip my skirts into the air with her walking cane as she vowed, "If Annie Laurie does not make your dresses longer, you are going to die with side pleurisy." She always made this calamitous prediction whenever I stood revolving in front of her bedroom's open fire on the first chilly days of fall.

Grandma's walking stick hitting against my skirts would make me think about another one of Uncle John's rhymes. "When I go out to promenade, I look so sweet and gay, I have to take a walking stick to keep the boys away!" Since Grandma used her walking stick to chastise me, I wanted to ask her if she had ever needed a sturdy cane in her younger days to "keep the boys away!" It was hard for me to visualize Grandma Phifer as a young girl. As long as I had known her, she was short, fat, and walked with a cane.

As a teenager she rode and kept a horse at the boarding school she attended in an adjoining county. I could not picture my mother on a horse. Grandpa Phifer kept a horse named Claybanks for his children to ride. however Claybanks would not let anyone but males saddle her. One day Mama dressed in one of her brother's clothing, went to the barn, and walked up to Claybanks with her saddle while saying in a gruff voice, "Here, Claybanks." Claybanks bit her hand and that ended Mama's attempt at being an equestrienne.

I thoroughly enjoyed growing up surrounded by aunts, uncles, great aunts, great uncles, and cousins by the dozens. As this was a time when older family members stayed in their homes instead of moving to retirement places, older relatives were always on hand to teach us to recite cute ditties and wise sayings. At an early age, I learned that a "whistling girl and a crowing hen will always come to some bad end." I never could whistle but along with my brother Thomas and sister Beatrice, we did come to some bad ends that prompted my mother to turn into a stern disciplinarian.

At these times, my mother took action with a keen switch. As she entered the room, flaying her denuded peach branch (with a few leaves left on at the tip to give added sting), we three culprits let out an instantaneous howl. We raced to the corners of the room and crouched on our knees to protect our naked legs, leaving our backs to bear the brunt of the licks. From the moment my mother flashed her weapon, we screamed and shrieked with such a ruckus that our mother never struck her first blow. The louder we yelled, the more fervidly she would plead with us to "Please hush before the neighbors hear your racket!" She was afraid they would think she was heartlessly abusing her fatherless children.

Any lag in the children's health, such as a cold lingering too long, according to the mutual agreement of our advisory board, needed to be taken care of with a strong dose of castor oil. This decision always brought forth my red-headed Aunt Alda, my single aunt who had stayed on at home to be with Grandma Phifer. She eagerly came first to lend a helping hand administering the medication. Before doling out the required dose, she would grab us with spirited hands and drag us out from under beds where we had taken refuge.

My determined mother and hot tempered Aunt Alda worked as a well rehearsed team in order to accomplish their mission. While one of them held us by the nose, the other poured down our opened mouths and throats doses of castor oil camouflaged with orange juice. This was an ordeal for them as well as for us. We really worked them into a fit, especially my peppery Aunt. In fact, the castor oil rarely went down into the proper organs because we raised such a hullabaloo that it did not have a working chance. To this day, I do not think the devil deserves a dose of castor oil with or without orange juice.

During our adolescent days, the menacing threat of an orphanage hung over our heads. The potential of my mother sending us to one filled our thoughts with fear and made us earnestly strive to be good children. My thrifty mother impressed upon us the necessity of frugal practices by taking us to a traveling tent show, "Over The Hills To The Poor House." This tear-jerker made us half-orphans sob from beginning to end. The thought of our mother going "Over The Hill" to a poor house, and we three children to an orphanage, incited so much dread in our youthful minds that the imminent threat of going to either place was enough to make us act like model children.

As model children, we were raised with religion playing a large part in our childhood. My brother Thomas frequently played the role of preacher, and my sister and I and our friends often served as his congregation. Thomas' favorite pulpit was the tin-covered rooftop of our wood shed. Whenever my mother was at work and a bad storm came up, Thomas would mount his high pulpit on bended knees, and fervently pray for the lightning and thunder to go away. When my mother discovered Thomas's elevated church position during thunderstorms, she put a stop to his prayers on top of a tin roof. "Tin roofs and heights," she pointed out, "draw lightning." That put a stop to the aspirations of Thomas to the ministry. Although preacher-struck, he wanted nothing to do with being struck by lightning.

My mother's family has always loved playing games, including card games such as finch, rook,and set back. Auction bridge came along when I was twelve, and I was adept enough to fill in as a fourth with adults. One day some of our young friends were playing cards with us when our minister called at the door. Finding my sister and me at the card table, he admonished us for playing cards instead of doing house work while our mother was working. Beatrice was so overcome with guilt that she took the cards into the backyard and set fire to them. I did not share the extent of her guilt and hurriedly rescued the "playing cards," as bridge cards were called at the time, before they were burned beyond use.

At times, we children were fostered out among my mother's extended family. During the last time we were scattered and enrolled in different schools, Thomas developed pneumonia for the third time. I was nine years old and was living with my Aunt Ede at Castle Point, New York, where Uncle Joe Rothman was a doctor with the Veterans Administration Hospital. (By coincidence, this same VA hospital has now become a center for the treatment of spinal cord injuries.)

While I was in New York, Beatrice was staying with Uncle Cliff and Aunt Blanche Jenkins in Lowell, North Carolina, a town located 15 miles from Bessemer City. Thomas was with Grandma Phifer and Aunt Alda in Bessemer City, and my mother was enrolled at Gaston Business College, where she was taking a secretarial course which would turn her into a full-time working mother. Grandpa Phifer said every family should have at least one "lady," and he selected Mama to be ours. Although Mama did not work in her youth, she said she had to forget the "Lady" image because the older she became, the harder she had to work.

For Thanksgiving that fall, my mother and Thomas went to Lowell to be with Beatrice and the Jenkins. During the holidays, he developed pneumonia with his condition so serious he could not be taken to a hospital. Mama had a Lowell doctor and a registered nurse to care for him. All during his illness, my mother was pessimistic about his recovery. Recalling the Ole Wives Tale that said having the third case of pneumonia was fatal, she feared the worst.

The worst happened. On December 8, 1928, my brother died.

Coming back to North Carolina for my brother's funeral, I remember events rather than any feeling of sadness. Aunt Ede and I came from New York by train. Another train caused a wreck ahead of us, which delayed our arrival. This resulted in the funeral being postponed by one day.

The hearse carrying my brother's body from Lowell to where the services were being held in Bessemer City had a flat tire, which delayed the funeral another hour. I can remember riding with Mama and Beatrice in the family car provided by the funeral home. As we sat in heavy traffic in Gastonia where the flat occurred, I can recall how bright and warm the day seemed while we waited for the tire to be changed. When we arrived in Bessemer City at the Presbyterian Church, the friendly sun had disappeared to be replaced by late afternoon shadows.

Mama, Bea and I walked through a formation of uniformed Boy Scouts standing on either side of the church entry. A Boy Scout ceremony was used with Thomas' casket flanked by flags of the United States, Boy Scouts of America, and the Christian flag. Thomas had just joined a Cub Scout pack that summer and was a friend to both Cub and Boy Scouts.

The Boy Scout service was the first I had ever seen, and I have never seen nor heard of it being used since that day in December of '28 when it was used for my only brother's funeral. The church was packed with both adults and students. Thomas' fifth grade classmates sat in a body. Crowds of people stood outside the church since the small sanctuary would not hold all who came. The death of a young person disturbs all ages. This was evident at Thomas' funeral.

In a detailed and elaborate obituary carried in the Gastonia Gazette under the caption, "Bessemer City Department," the correspondent stated, "Tuesday afternoon at three o'clock the Presbyterian Church was packed, all standing places being taken, for the funeral of Thomas Phifer Sexton, 11-year-old son of Mrs. Annie Phifer Sexton." The article listed the order of service with all the ministers in town having a part. The obituary even mentioned the details of my father's accidental death.

Coming from Castle Point for my brother's funeral, I was too young to fully understand the absolute sadness of his death. My adolescent, self centered mind was too busy wondering if my hometown friends had noticed I was wearing silk breeches. Before, my mother usually made my panties out of the same materials she made my dresses. Wearing silk ones was something new and wonderful to me, especially in winter time. Aunt Ede's house on the VA hospital grounds was steam heated, which meant there was no need for long underwear. Always conscious of my new underwear, I tried to sit so that my silk pants would show, only slightly.

I also wanted to be sure to let my Southern friends know that I was taking dancing lessons in Newburgh, New York, and to get there, I had to cross the Hudson River on a ferry, which was a new and exciting weekly event for me. What made my excitement even more intense was my Aunt Ede's habit of falling asleep when she was seated. She even took wee naps at the bridge table, but always managed to be the high scorer.

She snoozed while we waited in line to drive on and off the ferry, which always made me hold my breath for fear she would still be half asleep and would drive us into the Hudson River. Riding with my aunt on trolleys also put my stomach into knots because as soon as we were seated, Aunt Ede would go to sleep while I sat there fretting over the prospects of missing our trolley stops. It was miraculous how when we neared our intended destinations, Aunt Ede always jerked awake just in time to ring the bell at the right locations.

Wearing silk pants, taking dancing lessons, and riding ferries and trolleys were all so different from the life I led in my hometown that I never got homesick. I felt big because I was going to school "up North." I can recall incidents from dancing lessons, but the only thing I can remember about my fourth grade schooling in the north was my teacher, who was so fat she had to walk down the aisles between our desks sideways.

Each time I saw her "sidewaysing" down an aisle, I thought that at home her derriere would be a disaster zone for pranksters. I could visualize my fat Yankee teacher going between the desks of my classroom at Bessemer City's West School, sliding one foot sideways at a time and saying "Hand."

Down South, with our hands stuck out in front of us and our fingers spread apart, the teacher would check for "itch." Itch and head lice were common juvenile afflictions during the Depression. If an examination of our hands brought evidence of an itchy rash, that meant a note home to our parents. With yellow sulfur crystals mixed in lard being the stock home remedy, we could smell our classmates under its cure, especially when the temperature rose. During these check ups I remembered my mother quoting the axiom, "It's not a sin to have itch. It is a sin to keep it!" Our family never sinned in that respect.

Next would come our southern teacher's order, "Head." That meant we had to lower our heads for a lice hunt. Some of my classmates called them "cooties." Most people who suffered head lice used kerosene to kill the nits. The hands and head checks were among the things I missed in my northern school. Down South, the roomful of children grew united in extending sympathy to the student under examination. We gave a unanimous sigh of relief as a student was declared "clean."

One thing I remember keenly about the North is that I had my first experience with prejudice and discrimination. Knowing I was a poor Southern orphan relative of my Aunt Ede, mothers on the VA post did not readily take to my associating with their daughters. When Uncle Joe enrolled me in the fourth grade in Beacon, N.Y., the school administration tried to put me back a grade because I was from the South and that meant I was ignorant. Uncle Joe took care of seeing that I was placed in my right grade level and my dimples soon made me the pet of the VA families.

In addition to being the pet of the VA families, I was the best dressed young girl in my group. Along with buying my clothes, Aunt Ede could sew, and not having any daughters of her own, she used her talents making me dress after dress. I remember the burst of pride I felt when I stood at my closet door and seeing all my beautiful dresses hanging there I thought, "These are all mine!"

I came home for my brother's funeral wearing silk breeches but not speaking with a Yankee accent. With frequent practices in an empty room and in front of a three way mirror, I could never affect a "Naw- thun" accent. I just could not catch onto the technique of making Bessemer City, North Carolina, come out in any other sound then "Bess-smur Sit-ee, Nath-kah-linah." Each word came out a syllable short. I could not shake the South out of my speech.

Returning to Bessemer City that summer, I realized for the first time that with Thomas' death, Mom, Bea and I were now a family of females. My mother had to take on the added duties of being a big brother as well as a father and mother to Bea and me.

How my mother must have hated to give up her only son, just a boy, a youth who had already earned the respect and love of both old and young. I know my brother's death was a most grievous loss for my mother, I never saw my mother cry or brood in despondency over losing Thomas or my father. She never let me see any tears fall over my later condition. The "lady" training came through helping her be reserved in her emotions, a trait I eventually had to adopt. Although she hid her sadness, I know she felt it deeply.

After my mother's death in May of 1964, among her things we found letters my father had written to her when they were courting, and different sentimental mementos she had kept through the years but never discussed. In the attic, we found a box containing woodwork pieces made by my brother, crayon pictures he had drawn on some of his school papers, his Cub Scout uniform, and the newspaper account of his death. Like the box, my mother kept sadness locked in her heart.

After I had grown to the age where orphanages and Old People's Homes stood for places of friendly refuge rather than places of horror, the thought of being the source of ever bringing tears to my mother held me in check. To me she was the Griselda of the 20th Century. Love, I try to teach my children, is the most wonderful thing in the world. Of all the numerous types of love, next to God's, what could be more comforting than a mother's love?

As I grew older, I appreciated my mother's love and care more and more as she devoted her life to her children, now reduced to two daughters.

Beatrice, Mama, and Lois

2

Chapter Two

Even though I lost my father and my only brother at an early age, I had a happy childhood as I grew up surrounded by females. With our family now reduced almost by half, life for Beatrice and me was still filled with love and laughter. Along with loving us, our mother did her best to give my sister and me the advantages that at times seem to mean more to mothers than to their offspring, such as piano and dancing lessons. Mama went one art further and added "expression" lessons, which meant we learned recitations and delivered them with exaggerated voices and gestures. Even the teacher gave up on this one, quitting after her first year.

It would have been to my advantage if my expression teacher had continued just a little bit longer to polish up my speaking. I do speak with an expressive voice but it is one that is high pitched when excited and loud when I am upset. All I remember now about my expression lessons is my teacher because she was so fat she waddled when she walked in any direction.

I had voice lessons free with my public schooling under a subject called Music Appreciation. I remember my voice teacher because at times she wore skin tight dresses that showed the imprint of her navel. She also wore a ring on her index finger, which I always admired as she directed our singing with that finger. In her low country of South Carolina accent, she would request us to sing "like buds."

My piano lessons remained a "must" according to my mother, and dancing lessons remained a "must" according to me, so I took both during my secondary schooling. Without hesitation,

I was always ready to admit that I preferred tapping my toes more than I did tapping the keys on a piano.

My dancing teachers left a more vivid impression on me than my other cultural instructors. They were different because, to me, they symbolized glamour and excitement. But, I have to admit, they did have a few idiosyncrasies. One dance instructor had stuck her head too near a heater to dry her hair rolled in celluloid curlers. The curlers caught on fire and burned portions of her scalp. Consequently, she wore a partial wig. Another aspect of this particular teacher, according to my mother, was, "She has no sense of modesty." When our dance group danced at public functions and students and dance instructors shared the same dressing room, she walked among us in bra and step-ins while puffing on her cigarettes.

Females, while I was growing up, dressed behind closed doors. She was the first woman I ever saw "naked."

Another dance teacher's teeth did not develop correctly so she had beautifully capped teeth, the first ones I ever saw up close. Every time she smiled, all I could see were rows of dollar bills because the rumor was she had paid a fortune for those perfect teeth. I marveled at her bright gold hair that stayed in perfect Marcelled waves, no matter how vigorously the dance steps were that she performed.

It seems in my youth that I always took note of and remembered the peculiarities about people's personalities and appearances. But in recalling piano recitals, it is my own peculiarities I remember most. Piano recitals for me were disasters because I simply could not memorize. Instead of playing the piano at recitals, the teacher had me recite while she played background piano selections for my musical readings. My senior year in high school, my teacher made me play a piece on the piano from memory at the spring recital. Terrified over playing in public, my mind went blank as I fumbled along, playing Page One over three times before striking a concluding chord. My mother, sitting in the audience, beamed with pleasure. She never could see anything wrong about "her baby," even my terrible piano performances. But that was Mama -- always behind me, ready to push me along.

Mama did not have to do any pushing to get me to perform in dance recitals. My youthful mind thought that they were the most wonderful things I had ever participated in. I could not have been any more elated over taking part in an opening night on Broadway than I was over getting to be in the lineup of dancers at our recitals. To me they were magnificent -- beautiful costumes, lighting effects, and a packed auditorium to perform to. While piano recitals were free, dance recitals were not. Everyone had to pay except the dancers. To be sure all paid, the teachers posted a ticket collector backstage to catch mothers sneaking in with their daughters and costumes. People were cagy with their money during Depression years.

Caroline Mauney, one of my best friends, and I took our lessons in Gastonia. In addition to needing money to pay for our lessons, we needed transportation. These problems worked themselves out. Since Caroline and I were quick to learn and could lead the line, our teachers gave us one free lesson a week. The teachers also gave another Bessemer City girl free lessons in exchange for her mother piling us into her Model A Roadster to transport us back and forth to Gastonia. Since the girl's father worked in Gastonia, he joined our group for the return trip home, making it a tight squeeze for two adults and three dancers to fit into a one seater car.

To pay for the remaining costs of dancing lessons, Caroline and I taught students in Bessemer City. I don't know what our Gastonia dance teachers would have thought of our teaching Bessemer City students dance routines we had learned in their classes for twenty-five cents a lesson. We had older students and younger ones, male and female. To top it off, we used the homes of our students for our dance studios, having different groups to meet at the different homes of our pupils.

Caroline and I not only cheated on our Gastonia teachers, we copied dance routines from any source we could. When I was 14 years old, a marvelous thing occurred: I saw the ocean for my first time. Aunt Ede and Aunt Pearl took me and several girls my age with them to a house party at Myrtle Beach, South Carolina. I was more fascinated by the dancers from the Henderson School of Dance from Charlotte, North Carolina, than I was by the ocean. The Henderson dancers spent summers at the beach. They practiced dance routines in the mornings for shows they put on at nights during dances held at the pavilion. Caroline and I watched their practices, which were free to the public. We never did get to see the final performances during the night time shows where admission was charged. We memorized their steps and routines, and when we returned home Caroline and I taught them to our students.

While Aunt Ede Rothman and Aunt Pearl Doyle took me to the ocean for my first time, Aunt Blanche Jenkins and Uncle John Hunter Phifer paid for Bea and me to attend summer camps. One summer we attended a camp in the mountains where we stayed in a building used in winters as a school dormitory. I cannot remember where the school was located, but I do remember prior to making our bunk beds for the first time, we were cautioned to look for bedbugs in the mattresses. None was discovered in our search and I forgot all about such insects existing, but not my sister, who was always the one in our family to concentrate on the minute details. In later years, after I was injured, she became a super bed bug searcher. This talent developed during our travels. Because of their convenience to my crippled condition, we were early customers at tourist courts.

These early tourist cabins were just that -- crude cabins usually lined up behind gas stations on the outskirts of towns. Stopping for the night at a tourist cabin made Beatrice have a sudden recall about our youthful bedbug searches. When we stopped at one as prospective customers, my sister, now our official insect searcher, checked the mattresses out while my mother inspected the bathroom facilities. Bea never did produce any bedbugs in her inspections but she did produce ill feelings, along with Mama, on the part of cabin managers, who gave us looks that said, "If you are that prissy, go on and pay the price for hotel accommodations."

While my sister consistently handled our lives in an orderly manner, I did things haphazardly. Since childhood I had been flighty and impulsive while my sister was steady. I was constant motion. I literally ran every minute of the day. When I awakened early in the mornings, I was eager to jump out of bed to get started making my rounds of activities.

I now tell people I had done enough walking and running in my youth to last me a lifetime.

I loved to dance, swim and play tennis but could not excel in a single one. About the only thing I could do well was to scheme various ways to get out of doing house work, and since I was "her baby," Mama let my schemes become successful efforts. Because I was her "little sister," Bea babied me, too, but with more sternness.

Our biggest work days were when my mother, now working for a power and light company, came home in the afternoons from work. Then she herded Bea and me to the woodshed in the backyard where our dirty clothes had been soaking in tin wash tubs. This area is now referred to as the "laundry room" in most homes. No matter what the place you do it in is called, washing clothes will always mean pure drudgery to me.

Before I was pushed to the back lot, I wrote a note to tack onto our front screen door stating, "Help. I am in the wood shed washing clothes. Rescue me!" That note was for any of my friends who came to our door and were inventive enough to manufacture excuses for getting me away from the wash pot.

That iron wash pot. How I hated standing over it to stir our clothes as they boiled in soapy water. As I stirred, I kept imagining all the fun things I was missing out on with my friends. I always hated the thought that I was not with my crowd when they were having fun, a feeling that lasted throughout my teenage years.

Time, however, changed my thoughts about the iron wash pot. The iron container that I once detested is now considered a treasured family possession that we have kept through the years to remind us of "The days when....."

Our family not only washed our own clothes, we also raised our own fryers in a chicken lot and grew our own vegetables in a garden plot. Raising chickens and growing vegetables turned out to be brief ventures. The chickens went first when a neighbor's dog got into our lot and killed the entire flock. Mama decided raising chickens was not for city life. Her yearn to grow vegetables outlasted the one to raise poultry.

When the first warm days of spring arrived, Mama's annual planting urge would hit her to put in a garden. This urge sent her mule hunting. Through the years the pickings grew sparse finding a man who owned a mule living within plowing distance that Mama could hire to plow her rows. She was always successful in her hunts and I grew up listening to the sounds of "Gee" and "Haw."

These gardening attempts never amounted to full production because invariably a dry spell would come along at some point during the summer and dry up Mama's crop. Each time this happened, my mother would vow, "This is the last year I am going to try to have a garden." But with the first warm days the following spring, Mama would be out mule hunting again.

Along with her spunk and stubbornness, I did not inherit my mother's enthusiasm for gardening. I hated the losing fight with weeds. I did not mind work, to some degree, but I was too restless to stand in one spot chopping at weeds. It is a slow, monotonous process. However, I could owe my career as a newspaper writer to those weeds. As I ran around town on my daily rounds, I gathered bits of news and gossip. Later, I relayed my findings to Mama and Bea as they worked at cutting down weeds in Mama's garden. As they hoed, I talked fast and hard as I waved my hands in all directions and used exaggerated expressions to describe the accounts I had gathered.

While they chopped, they eagerly listened to my up-to-the-minute gossip. I always kept an ear out for the sensational, as I noticed at an early age that the unusual is the thing that piques interest in others. I also learned that the best news and features do not come to you, a news writer has to get out and sniff and hunt for the best news. And I was willing to hunt for it then just as I am now as a newspaper writer.

Becoming a working housewife and mother, I needed help from my entire family in order to function. I cannot complain about my two older children, Sam and Annette, when it comes to helping me with household chores. They have always been willing to help. But my baby daughter, Lisa, is cut from a different pattern -- mine! When I complain about Lisa's non-interest in house work, my sister Beatrice nods her head and smirkingly states, "Lisa is just what you deserve!"

By the time I became a teenager, Mama gave up on washing our own clothes and we turned that task over to paid help, and she switched her gardening interest from vegetables and flowers to flowers exclusively. The step from the wash shed and garden into high school, that included grades eighth through eleventh, turned into Big Doings for me because three major things occurred which placed me apart from my classmates: an appendicitis operation, a tonsillectomy, and nearsightedness. I loved being in a crowd but I did not conform to the crowd. I grew up wanting to be different. I just did not want to be a blind follower.

With appendicitis, I was the only student in the entire high school to have an appendix removed that school year. I was not the only one to get rid of my tonsils, but the technique used to remove mine was different. I had mine done locally with my tonsils frozen for the surgery. As for my eyeglasses, I was not the only student to wear them in my school but I was the only one to have pink shell rimmed spectacles.

All three events held a bearing on my future. My two operations let me know what life was like being sick and hospitalized, and my glasses, at first a joy, turned into what I later thought was my nemesis when I became a college student.

The place and time for my appendicitis pains to strike, coupled with my flighty nature, almost did me in. I was sitting in church and the First Presbyterian congregation had started singing a slowed-down tempo of "Bringing In The Sheaves" prior to taking up collection when my first severe pain struck. My acute pains produced much whispering behind the hymnals between my mother and me, with my imploring whispers being the more forceful as I repeatedly moaned, "My stomach is killing me!" My mother kept frowning and sending shushes in my direction.

After many pain-prompted groans by me, my mother eventually allowed me to do a most uncommon thing, get up and leave service while collection was being gathered. I spent a miserable afternoon in pain while trying to convince my sister that I did hurt and that I was not pretending. Bea kept saying to me, "Stop faking, Lois. Help me with the dishes."

Although I was guilty of pulling a "cry wolf" illness before, the facts finally became established that "Lossie was stricken" with an ailment that needed professional diagnosing rather than our usual home counseling. Compared to most of today's doctor-patient relations, I hesitate to tell anyone how our family doctor rallied to my condition. I am afraid when I indulge myself in telling about "my first operation" and give details of how Dr. George Patrick came to my house to examine me, people will conclude, "This is another one of Lois' exaggerations."

Dr. Patrick, a family friend who looked after my health needs from childhood through years of paraplegia, after examining me, picked me up and carried me to his car to drive me the more than thirty-five miles to Mercy Hospital, a Catholic supported hospital in Charlotte, for further examinations. Reaching the hospital, he picked me up and carried me into the emergency room. He told my mother he feared my appendix was a time bomb that could explode any minute. He was right. I was admitted as an emergency patient.

Thinking back, I have drawn the conclusion that the necessity of my having to be carried into the hospital for my first stay must have been an omen of my future because I have been "toted" in and out of a number of different hospitals since that time.

My Aunt Pearl Doyle, a registered nurse, came to nurse me in the hospital. She never forgot an embarrassing incident for her that took place when the patient fared better than her nurse. The night after my surgery, as the saying goes, "the patient is doing as well as can be expected," was my case. However, Aunt Pearl, who at the time was a Veterans Administration nurse and had also served overseas during World War I as an army nurse, blacked out in a restroom. This left her terribly chagrined over creating more commotion than the patients on my ward. She never forgot keeling over in a hospital "john" and being saved by a nun.

Undergoing my first major surgery, I discovered that illness is not all bad. I was happy over the attention I received as boxes of letters were brought to me that had been written by my classmates who composed them during class. Their letters indicated cheer over the assignment of writing letters to me instead of doing routine studies. These letters also gave me advance notice that I was the envy of my class. I was anxious to get back to school to see this envy in person. How could postoperative gas pains compete with my anticipation of going home?

At the time of my first hospitalization, the Depression was eating away at everyone's pocketbooks. My mother still worked for the same power and light company, making a small salary. Dr. Patrick had done his part by letting the hospital administration and my surgeons know that my mother was a hard working widow with two growing daughters to support, and that their bills would be financial burdens to her. The usual fees were based on the patient's ability to pay.

Before I could be dismissed, my hospital bill had to be paid. Mama was of the school of thought that when a person worked, she worked. The idea never occurred to her to get off from work to come herself to get me from the hospital. When the time came to settle my accounts for my medical bills, my mother sent my sister to handle the finances.

Sister Bea blew it. Beatrice rode in the ambulance that would take me home. As a high school student, Beatrice had a flair for the theatrical. She took advantage of the occasion of getting me out of the hospital by putting on a show of Poor Girl Acting Rich. To play her role of guardian of Little Sister, Bea latched onto some of Aunt Pearl Doyle's wardrobe. Watching from my hospital bed as my dear sister made her grand entrance almost kept me in the hospital from shock. Bea stood there dressed as a pert flapper turned vamp. She wore a full length fur coat, silk stockings, spike heels, and a clutch hat with pearl ear bobs peeking out from it. Consequently, we did not come anywhere near the charity list prices for my first hospitalization.

After this first hospital experience, I got my introduction to the importance of saving for a Rainy Day Sick Fund. Little did I realize at that time that one day my medical expenses would turn from a light sprinkle to a "toad strangling" torrent.

To this day, all my medical expenses have had to come from family funds. From the Depression through the time of my auto accident, there were no such things as company health insurance plans or compulsory car liability insurance requirements. The truck with the faulty brakes which caused my crippling condition was a state owned vehicle. Therefore, no claim could be made against it because sovereign immunity from suits or damages protected the state. That left my family totally responsible for forty years, to date, of financing my medical care.

My appendix scar had barely healed before Beatrice had to serve as family agent seeing after my medical needs once again. When I had to have my tonsils removed, Bea left her starstruck acting at home to accompany me. She went with me on the morning train to Gastonia attired as a high school senior should. My doctor had his offices located a block from the railroad station in upstairs quarters over a drug store on main street.

An upstairs location for doctors in buildings without elevators seemed to be the "in" thing that continued up until after World War II. For my surgery, I sat in a dentist type chair that cranked up and tilted backwards for the doctor to gaze inside my throat. My tonsils were frozen with a local anesthetic for the doctor to put a metal wire contraption inside my throat to clip out my tonsils.

Since this was something new to Bea and me, Beatrice was allowed to stand behind the nurse, who was a pleasant black woman, to see the surgeon's technique. From her vantage point, Bea had full view of the procedures. Half way through the procedure, Bea, observing the doctor's bloody results, blacked out and hit the floor. She shared the bed reserved for my recovery where she lay supine while I tossed and turned, bored from inactivity. My tonsils were still frozen and I was feeling no pain.

Bed rest for both of us ended when it was time for the late afternoon train from Gastonia to Bessemer City. I could not wait for the local to make its Bessemer City stop so that I could run from friend's house to friend's house to show off and tell about my operation. I also wanted to find out if any major events had happened while I was in Gastonia. A whole day away from home seemed such a long time when I was growing up.

Back home from my rounds, and with the anesthesia worn off, I hurt, but not badly enough to keep me from talking to my friends who came by our house, some bringing ice cream. My tonsillectomy recovery turned into a mini party when I served ice cream to my callers. My tonsil hurt was way in the background because foremost in my thoughts were the new Chinese-style pajamas I wore during my recuperation. I even wore them when male schoolmates came for visits.

My second experience with illness and operations reaffirmed my first concept that sickness was indeed not all that bad. Poor health at times can be something to enjoy, especially if you can work it right by getting enough attention. At this point, I felt satisfied I was getting my share.

That summer, I was fostered out again with Aunt Ede and Uncle Joe Rothman for the summer in Washington, D.C., where Uncle Joe had been transferred by the Veterans Administration. While I was staying with them, Uncle Joe took my cousin Phifer Rothman and me to see Barnum Brothers Circus. Uncle Joe became alarmed when he noticed I couldn't see the high trapeze performers. He was even more alarmed when I could not make out President Herbert Hoover sitting just a short distance away in his circus box. Suspecting my trouble, Uncle Joe took me to an eye specialist who confirmed Uncle Joe's suspicion that I was nearsighted. I only saw half of what I should. The result of this disclosure meant that when I returned to Bessemer City for the fall school term, I was proudly wearing a pair of pink shell rimmed glasses. I was thrilled with their appearance and was happy they were not black rimmed spectacles like the ones my school friends wore.

Starting back to school that fall without tonsils or appendix and wearing pastel-colored rimmed glasses, I really was different. From proceeds from a rummage sale which my girlfriend Caroline and I had conducted as a joint financial project, I got my first electric permanent wave. My mother did not mind my spending money for a permanent but she did get a little vexed when she found out I had sold some of my best clothes in the rummage sale.

Now back in school, wearing a long appendix scar and my pink-rimmed glasses along with my new frizzed hairstyle, I thought I truly must be right there with my movie idol, Clara Bow, when it came to having "it." Looking back, my idea of having "it" was immature and was restricted to rolling my eyes up and down in a cha-cha-cha fashion as I uttered "Ooh la lahs." Pathetic as my imitations were, I still considered myself the Cat's Meow.

Sexton ladies strike oil

3

Chapter Three

As the time neared for my high school graduation, our family council did not have the chance to decide if I went to college or not. Fate made the decision. College for me had been a debatable issue because my mother felt hesitant over spending her savings on a probable failure. Academically, I had never made my mother's pride expand as my sister had done. At the time I received my high school diploma, Beatrice had graduated with honors from Lees McRae Junior College in Banner Elk, North Carolina, and was in the process of transferring from the University of Tennessee in Knoxville to Agnes Scott College near Atlanta.

Before Mama had decided about college or not for me, I was blasted into higher education by a gush of oil. What my family had dreamed about since the year I was born happened in the spring of 1936: an oil boom gushed forth on our Louisiana property.

When the oil leases were signed in July of 1935, Mama sold some of her mineral rights in order to insure that she would have sufficient funds to pay college costs for her daughters. Before signing our leases, a lot of drawn-out negotiations took place between Grandpa Sexton and the men interested in leasing the property. During this period, I went to stay with Beatrice at Banner Elk, where she worked in the library at Pinnacle Inn, which was what Lees McRae College became during the summer months.

The Inn boasted of being 4,000 feet in the air and as Bea and I speculated on the possibilities of oil riches, our expectations jumped another 4,000 feet into the air. Immediately following the "discovery" well in the Rodessa Field, wires from Rodessa to Bessemer City became an almost everyday event.

My grandfather's brother, Uncle Robert Sexton, served as the Sexton family wire sender. After a lifetime of frugality, Uncle "Sec," turning into a rich man, continued to send his cryptic style messages through the wire service's ten word limit. His messages were short but sweet: "Sexton Number One a gusher. Number Four spudded in. Love, Robert."

With oil flowing in our direction, my family's thoughts became soaked in it. Overnight, we turned into amateur mineralogists as we eagerly waited for other wells to come in on our oil pool. Our joys mixed with anticipation, and excitement became touched with giddiness, as Uncle Sec's telegrams kept coming in: "Sexton Number Eleven. Oil saturated," etc.

As each rig neared pay dirt, we kept our fingers crossed that no salt water would show and that when the Big Blow did come, it would be slimy black instead of the grayness of natural gas. Natural gas was so inexpensive that our family would have made more money planting cow peas. When the field was brought in, no pipelines had been constructed so the natural gas that came out with the petroleum was directed into slush pits where it was burned. Flares leaped high in the air and could be seen for miles, especially at night when they turned the sky into a fiery glow.

From the moment the leases had been signed, speculators had flocked to the Rodessa Field where they frantically tried to buy in on the chances that the field would be a producing one. And when it was, oil speculators and politicians became as excited as Beatrice and I over the Visions of Riches.

In addition to receiving wires from Uncle Sec, Mama received them from other people who were anxious to buy a percentage of her mineral rights. Some even flew to our door trying to persuade her to sell more of her royalties. Fortunately, due to Beatrice's and my status as minors, we were able to hold onto our full royalty shares in spite of high handed pressures placed on my mother.

At that time we had sold our 60 acres of the 100 acres of land that my Daddy bought the year I was born, but had retained 51 percent of its mineral rights.

In those days, when it came to oil, anything went whether it was legal or not. As a new oil royalty owner, Mama wasn't naive about "hot oil" deals that in those days were major scandals in the oil boom fields. But she and Grandpa Sexton were powerless to handle them. It seemed that a lot of people were getting "pieces of the petroleum pie" with everybody getting rich but us Sextons.

Grandpa Sexton had always been a hold-out when it came to getting money for his property and goods. As a planter, when cotton did not bring in a good price, he stored his until it did. When oil developers started trailing him, wanting to lease his and our property, he held out in order to lease the Sexton oil pool to more than one developer. He waited one out until he got what he wanted. It turned out Grandpa's foresight worked to our benefit. He leased the Sexton land, in which our immediate family holds a sixth interest, to W.H. Hunter; our forty acres to Pelican Oil; and the sixty acres we still held mineral rights to went to the Ardis Company.

Our forty acres, lying in the heart of the Rodessa Field, became the most productive of the entire field. The Hunter leases used old pipes from another oil field. Eventually, these pipes rusted so badly they couldn't be pulled out of the ground. In a sad turn of events, our wells on the Hunter lease had to be abandoned while they were still producing in the late 1960's. The Pelican Company used good equipment and several of their wells on our 40 acres are still producing over forty years later, but it is sold at the low rate classified as "old oil."

It was the Pelican lease of our 40 acres that created a furor among oil men in Louisiana, Texas, Oklahoma, and eventually Washington, D.C. Our 13 wells in the Pelican lease were featured almost daily in newspaper reports of oil and gas from

March 21 to June of 1936. The thing that made the case unique was the reports of the past of our country's exploitation of oil resources. During this time, 150,000 known barrels of our oil were shipped with only the knowledge that they were "shipped overseas."

The mysterious case started when Dr. J.A. Shaw, director of minerals for the Louisiana Conservation Department, apparently on his own gave an order of "extra allowable" to the Pelican Company, stating that the company could run 20,000 barrels of oil per day from our 13 wells for 60 days or longer. This was at a time when the state conservation department, headed by Dr. Shaw and backed by Louisiana Governor James A. Noe, had prorated production of each well in Louisiana to be limited to producing 350 barrels per day. Dr. Shaw's order to Pelican permitted each one of our 13 wells to produce 1,537 barrels of oil a day for 60 days or longer while all other wells in the state, including the Rodessa Field, were each limited to 350 barrels per day. Pelican was selling the oil to the East Texas Refinery Company.

Dr. Shaw's order, which he stood behind all through the different tender board hearings and courts, created anger among the Rodessa Field oil developers and among oil men in other oil producing states who were afraid the extra allowable would cause oil prices to drop.

Our wells being allowed to over-produce meant that pressures in the surrounding wells were lessened and that salt water would develop and eventually the entire field would be ruined. On the fourth day, when our wells had run off 80,000 barrels of crude, oil developers and oil field workers in the Rodessa Field staged a mob scene to protest Pelican's extra allowable production. Their protests stopped the wells from producing for a period.

Meanwhile, the East Texas Pipeline Company laid a pipeline from our forty acres to Longview, Texas, where it tied in with the Tidewater pipeline that shipped petroleum to Gulf ports for shipment. When papers came to Mama for her to sign to give East Texas Pipeline permission to lay the pipeline on our land, it carried with it a message we interpreted as "You better sign this or else." The contract stated that if the pipeline was not laid, we would have to pay 20 cents per barrel for storage as long as the barrels holding our oil stayed on the Pelican lease.

Mama, for herself and for us as our guardian, quickly signed the papers agreeing to give right of way permission for the pipeline's construction. When our oil passed over into Texas, the Texas Railroad commission took up the battle of refusing to carry Louisiana oil from an extra allowable order into Texas.

U.S. Senator Tom Connally of Texas requested Federal authorities to look thoroughly into the situation, which grew into the U.S. versus East Texas Pipeline Company. Senator Connally said it was not fair to Texas oil developers to let extra allowable oil from Louisiana come into Texas when Texas wells were reduced to a "dribble." At that time, Texas conservation prorated each Texas well to producing 25 barrels of oil per day. Senator Connally also stated that he feared the result of this situation would bring the price of oil down.

Oil in 1936 was bringing $1.10 and $1.15 a barrel and was selling from our 13 wells for 85 cents a barrel at the well. Connally also pointed out the waste of natural gas as the result of the extra allowable. I remember Mama's "crying" over the fact that $4,000 in natural gas a day was being burned off in slush pits when the extra allowable oil was produced.

On May 21, 1936, Federal Judge Randolph Bryant placed a restraint on the movement of our oil into Texas, ruling that "the oil had not been produced validly or legally and is contraband oil, and channels of interstate commerce are denied it."

The 80,000 barrels of oil that had been produced in the four day period were impounded in Texas while Sen. Connally asked Harold Ickes, U.S. Secretary of the Interior, to investigate the case. George W. Holland, director of the U.S. Interior's conservation division, made a ten day trip to look into the Pelican

situation on our forty acres. He recommended to Secretary Ickes that "the extra allowable oil going from the Pelican lease in
Louisiana to Texas was not the potential source of contraband
oil it appeared to be." Secretary Ickes accepted Holland's rec-
ommendation and scratched our 13 wells off the "hot oil" list,
but said he would give the situation continued attention.

When the extra allowable oil started to flow again, our immediate family was as unhappy as other oil men were in the field.
Because of our interest in other Sexton wells on surrounding
leases, Pelican's extra oil allowable was endangering our hold-
ings. As mysteriously as the order was given, production of the
extra allowable stopped before the "60 days or longer" period.

A year later, a Kilgore (Texas) reporter tried to find out the
destination of the shipment of our 140,000 barrels of oil, which
included the 80,000 barrels that were impounded. When state
and federal directors in the petroleum industry were asked, they
passed the buck to one another, with none of them divulging to
what country the oil had been shipped.

The Kilgore newspaper said the oil was reportedly shipped to
Italy. If our oil had been shipped to Italy, it makes interesting
speculations. When Dr. Shaw gave his order for Pelican's extra
allowable, Premier Benito Mussolini had invaded Ethiopia and
our oil could have been intended for the invasion. But our oil
became tied up as contraband until June of 1936, and by that
time Italy had accomplished its mission of annexing Ethiopia.

Adding further thought to this, the extra allowable stopped
being in effect after June of 1936, and did not extend into its
60 day or longer period as the order had stated. The petroleum
from our 13 wells was supposedly high grade petroleum that
was desirable for aircraft engines.

Also holding interest to me is that riches from minerals had
been a dream on both sides of my family. The ancestors of my
mother's father, Junius Leroy Phifer, were mineral owners when
they migrated to America. The Phifers in Europe had been

granted mining rights to nine copper mines in Berne, Germany. My Grandpa Phifer spent his lifetime prospecting for minerals in the Bessemer City area, as well as in parts of upper South Carolina, but what mineral rights he did manage to buy expired long before minerals started to be mined again in the area on a large scale.

My mother shared her father's interest in minerals and completed his paperwork. At different times I had heard her mention sending off "Papa's samples" to be assayed. Grandpa Sexton was luckier than my Grandpa Phifer. By living to be 97 years old, he lived long enough to see his dreams come true. He thoroughly enjoyed turning from a planter into an oil man.

When we Sextons did turn into oil property owners, our family found out that most people think when oil gushes forth from a little worthless piece of land, money falls into the lessor's hands so fast that, without taking time out to count it, he dashes off to buy a Cadillac and a ticket to Paris or some other fun spot. Regretfully, it is only the lessee and oil developers who can afford such delightful actions.

With our oil income, my mother did stop working, we did build a larger house, we did buy our first car, a 1936 Dodge, and we did take off for a trip, going to Louisiana to look at the phenomenon that had taken place down on Grandpa's farm. Seeing our oil field under development for the first time was indeed a thrilling experience, like seeing a Christmas wonderland for real. We arrived at night, and miles before reaching Rodessa, we could see the glowing red reflections of natural gas flares as they burned in the slush pits. The drilling rigs were strung with lights from top to bottom so that the roustabouts could continue drilling during the night. The tower shaped derricks, with their strings of white lights, made the field look as if it were dotted with Christmas trees. As property owners, Mama, Bea and I were permitted to go through the gates fencing off the oil derricks and posted with "No Trespassing" signs.

We stood on the platforms with the roustabouts and saw how fast they could handle pushing the drill bits down with long pipe casings. I took guarded looks at the roustabouts because I had always thought they were rough and tough. To me, they looked like strong men who were serious about doing their work, and were not the menacing devil-may-care types the early movies had made them out to be.

I never did have the thrill of being present when the swab was drawn from a casing of a well we owned so I could see oil, water, and mud shoot above the derrick as a gusher. This would have been a thrilling sight for me. When a well comes in, the drillers let the well gush into the air until all the water and mud in the casing are gone before a valve is turned to send the oil into storage tanks. From a gauge on a well, while the oil is gushing into the air, the number of barrels it will produce per day can be estimated. This determines whether or not a well is termed a "gusher." Most of our wells shot out enough oil into the air to be gauged as gushers.

Even before we had oil wells that spewed out as gushers in Louisiana, I always looked forward to visiting there. When we were young, the Sextons sent money for us to make summer visits with them. I now gasp remembering how our family made lengthy visits with relatives; we did not pack suitcases, we packed a trunk. Imagine having a widow with her three children arriving on your door steps today with a trunk full of clothes for an extended visit! Our relatives had to love us. They financed our trips, and when we left, we always left them in tears. Now I wonder if their tears had been ones of sadness over our departure or joy! I'll never know. Those relatives have passed on, taking with them a style of life that seems to be gone forever.

How I treasured our visits to Louisiana. Like the Phifers, the Sextons were a close knit family. In our youth the Sexton home, over a hundred years old and made with wooden pegs, had a wide hallway running through the middle of the first floor from front to back with matching steps leading onto it at either end. It was as though a wide open hallway had been built through the middle of the house on the first floor. This style of architecture was used because of summer heat and wind storms. Tornadoes and cyclones had hit the area several times. A two-minute tornado hit in February of 1938 after the field was in full production killing twenty people and injuring forty others in the small settlement. One well caught fire and ran wild, threatening to explode the other wells, but the wind changed direction, which saved the field.

I might very well owe my life to that wind change. If the field had suffered, my family would not have had the money to finance my expensive medical bills after I was injured.

One thing that held interest for us North Carolina youngsters was a dug-out, rock-walled storm pit in the yard, where we would climb down inside to seek shelter during windstorms. By the time our summer visits started, the storm pit had turned into a snake pit, so we stayed inside the house and took our chances there during wind storms.

Our young spirits went wild with imagination over other aspects about the house as well. Slave labor had built it, and our young Louisiana cousins fascinated us, and scared us too, with tales that a slave had been left chained inside the walls. At nights in our beds, as we would lie there terrified, one of our cousins would quietly whisper, "I hear him!" In the quietness, the rest of us would claim we too heard the slave, as he stalked inside the walls pulling his chains along behind his shackled legs as he walked.

Grandpa Sexton's parents were opposed to owning slaves, which did not make them popular with the Ku Klux Klan, and for that reason, they had to flee from South Carolina, to Louisiana to make their home following the Civil War. Grandpa had inherited the Louisiana house through his wife's estate.

While the Sextons who immigrated to this country as Quakers

were non slave owners, my mother's grandparents, the Jacob Ramseurs, were the largest slave owners in their township in Gaston County, North Carolina, at the onset of the Civil War. Looking at the property listing for Crowders Mountain Township prior to the Civil War, I was appalled to see that slaves were listed by my ancestors like chattel, with their valuation based on the amount of work they produced. In the tax books, slaves were listed such as "Joe, age 27, $2,000; Mary, age 22, $1,500; John, age 5, $500; and his twin sister, Sarah, withered arm, $150."

The Sextons played low key roles in the Civil War while my mother's ancestors took prominent parts on my Grandmother Phifer's side of the family. Stephen Dodson Ramseur of Lincolnton, North Carolina, was, at 25, the youngest West Point General in the Confederate Army. The last meeting of the Confederacy took place at the William Phifer home in Charlotte where Judah P. Benjamin, Attorney General for the Confederate States and subsequently Secretary of State and Secretary of War, signed the last official papers for the Confederacy while a guest of the Phifers.

During the fighting and Reconstruction days, the majority of Ramseur slaves remained loyal to their owner. As a young girl, I still remember how frightened we children were when we walked by a patch of woods along a rural road on the Ramseur homeplace, where we had been told the slaves hid the family livestock when the Yankees came through. With my vivid imagination, I would think I heard the bridles of the horses clanking as I ran with bated breath past their hiding place in the woods.

I held my breath at Grandpa Sexton's house as I imagined other noises I could hear. Rumor was that ancestors of the Slaughters (my Grandmother's family) had hidden their gold and silver on the premises. Diggers were run off during the day, so they dug at nights in hopes of finding a treasure in coins.

Along with tales of ghosts, Yankees and treasure diggers, oil was a big topic for us Sexton kids when we were growing up.

Visiting in Louisiana, we North Carolina grandchildren were always announcing to Grandpa Sexton that we had found oil between the rows of cotton in his field. I just knew oil had to be there because, I wondered, what else would make the cotton grow so much higher than North Carolina cotton? I had heard about oil but not about delta cotton.

Grandpa Sexton always took our excited announcements of finding oil on his property in stride. Although he had a strong faith that oil was on his property, he knew it would not be discovered standing between his cotton rows; he knew it would have to be drilled for. As it turned out, to find our oil did take deep drilling. Our oil wells' "pay zones" were over a mile deep. Sexton No. 13 was cored in at 6,070 feet.

Becoming an oil lessor in his old age did not dim Grandpa's sense of humor. His wit sharpened as he aged. His humorous way of expressing himself kept his visitors quoting his witty sayings. From the first time I saw him, he was a wiry-built, white-headed man with a Van Dyke beard who fit the picture of a Southern gentleman who, in spite of his years, always rose gallantly from his chair to stand in the presence of females. He had two bachelor brothers-in-law, Robert and James Slaughter, who were in his age range. It was always a contest to see which of the three gentlemen would be the last to take a seat because all three conceded to each other's age and infirmities.

Grandpa suffered bad health in his middle life, and his children thought his death was imminent, a thought that prevailed for almost half a century. Each time we made a trip to see him, we figured it would likely be the last time we would see him alive. When Beatrice was first born, Mama and my Daddy took my sister to see Grandpa Sexton so he could see his first grandchild before he passed on. But, like me, Grandpa would not play dead. In his later years, he may have lost his sense of hearing and sight, but he did not lose his sense of humor. He laughed away his handicaps, a trait I desperately would need to inherit.

Lois and Agnes Scott classmates

4

Chapter Four

With oil money in the bank, college was within my means. Selecting a college became for me the hardest decision I had to make during my sixteen years. I did not stay in a quandary long, however, because Beatrice solved my problem. She always had a boyfriend and his place of higher education became her choice, too. When I was ready to enter college, Bea's boyfriend at the time was planning to study dentistry. When he transferred from the University of Tennessee to the dental school in Atlanta, Bea transferred with him to nearby Decatur where she enrolled at Agnes Scott. Not having any boyfriends to sway my emotions, I tagged along after my Big Sister, as I had always done, and Agnes Scott became for both of us our place of destiny. For Bea, it led to matrimony with a change of boyfriends, and it became a place of near fatality for me.

Getting admitted to Agnes Scott was not as easy as it sounds. I made it through its stately portals as a halfway student. Since I lacked a year of the four years of foreign language the college required for entry, I was termed an "irregular" student. That meant I did not belong to any class. I was just there. Just barely there, I have to admit; compared to the collection of brains at Scott, I was plumb dumb.

Fortunately my roommate, Anita Howard, shared my problems. Neither of us had enough of an academic background to even know how to walk in the Halls of Learning. We were crawlers surrounded by brain heavy joggers. We struggled to get a few minus grades with the required number of merit grades to pass.

My irregular classification did not keep me from falling in love with Agnes Scott and the City of Atlanta. At the drop of a token, I was ready to hop onto a trolley and rock along with it over its rough tracks to get into the heart of the city. My smalltown background made me feel cosmopolitan attending concerts at the Fox Theatre and eating at Chinese restaurants. When I found out at the end of my freshman year that I would have to spend my vacation months in summer school in order for me to return to Agnes Scott, I was delighted. I had feared my grades would have put me out of Scott for good.

I was more than willing to spend my first college summer making up the one year of foreign language I had needed for entering there in the first place, and also taking a summer college course to try for a merit grade to bring my scholastic score up to the required average.

To get readmitted for my second year, I took a summer school course at Davidson College, and private lessons in Latin taught by an elderly school teacher who lived in Bessemer City. Both of my summer school teachers were men.

Davidson College at that time was an all-male college, but several females were permitted to study there during the summer term. My professor, who was used to teaching a room full of males, always gave me the shifty eye look but not with a "dirty ole man" lecherous gleam. It was more with a "I wish she'd go away" look. I think he was dubious of my qualifications.

He turned out to be right. During the course, he popped an easy question to me: "Why does the United States celebrate the 4th of July?" As that simplest of simple questions passed to my corner in the back of the room, thirty pairs of male eyes turned to look in my direction with the level of their gazes focusing on my anatomy somewhat below my chin. Coming from an all-female home and an all-female college, I did not feel comfortable surrounded entirely by male eyes.

Sitting there blushing in my corner, the center of attention in a room full of the opposite sex, I defensively crossed my arms over my bosom and with all traces of intelligence blocked out of my mind, stammered, "I don't know." Consequently, at the end of the summer term, I received a failing grade. Seeing my bad grade, I did what I had always done in high school with male teachers. I burst into tears. With my failing grade in hand, I confronted the professor with loud sobbing and wailing as I made a massive effort to upgrade my report. Not being prepared to deal with precarious female emotions, the professor, with a confused expression, changed my grade. When I saw it was passing but not high enough to rate a Scott merit grade, I sort of toppled over into his direction and in an imploring wail, sobbed, "Can't you make it a 'B'?" He did to get rid of me and my squalling.

With my mission accomplished, I moved into Latin lessons which I took at the home of my teacher. Since his wife was away working at the hour of my instruction, I felt uneasy about being alone and shut away in a large house with an old man. I made it a point to always sit down on the wide front porch, rain or shine, to struggle through conjugating Latin verbs.

Something about that old guy made me suspicious. I made it a habit to arrange my chair to face the street where children, who were usually playing, could see me. After I had paid my teacher for the course, which automatically produced a passing grade, I later heard that the man was arrested for exposing himself, while standing on his front porch, to the children who played across the street. Even at college age, I had never heard about sexual perverts. But an innate sense of suspicion can vibrate warning signals to the innocent. The vibes signaled to me told me there was something odd about my Latin teacher.

With re-entry requirements met, I returned to Agnes Scott for the 1937-38 term. Not as a sophomore, as I had hoped, but again I was classified as an irregular student. After having gone through a summer of instructional endeavors, I felt I should have rated being termed a "special" student instead of irregular. It made me feel as though the college thought I was "second" quality. As an irregular, that meant that for the two years of my college education, my picture in the college annual was carried on the back page with foreign students who were enrolled at Scott for a year's study. I never made it from the back pages to be listed in a class in a college annual.

Tears could work on Davidson professors, but not on those steely-eyed female professors at Scott. During a student one-on-one conference, an English instructor directed her cold, unfeeling eyes on me, a nervous irregular sitting there quaking with uneasiness, and, using a classy intonation to her voice, she informed me, "You have made a number of egregious errors." Since she taught English, I thought she was referring to my grammar deficiency. But in the confinement of my limited vocabulary, I thought maybe she was referring to my having broken a Scott rule. Frustrated, I did not know whether to put on my smiling or my crying act.

Thrown into confusion, my mind leaped to an incident that had occurred that week when the assistant Dean had come to Anita's and my room; she left us shedding tears of remorse over her visit. Without properly signing out, the assistant Dean informed us, we had been seen that afternoon riding in a car with a a male. Under the double honor system followed at Scott, we had been reported by a fellow student for breaking a rule. What we had done was wrong because we were required to sign out with the Dean, along with the name of a male we would be with. The Dean had to approve the male for him to be on or off campus with any Agnes Scott girl. Later, after my tears were over, the only lasting regret I had from the incident was that I never found out which sanctimonious poop had reported us.

Bringing my mind back to the conference room, I soon realized it was my poor knowledge of English grammar that I was guilty of. During my college days I never did satisfactorily catch on to the mechanics of the English language. My college professors would no doubt shudder in disbelief if they learned I now make my living as a writer.

In my second year of college, I started making better grades, and scholastics stopped being my biggest problem. The thing that now gave me great pain was having to wear glasses. Objects that once set me apart from other students in my secondary school years were still setting me apart, but with the wrong look. With dismay, I realized my glasses made me look more bookish than interesting, even if they were pink-shell rims. I began to hate having to wear glasses. This was prompted by a Dorothy Parker witticism: "Men seldom make passes at girls who wear glasses."

This statement cut my sensitivity to the quick. Glasses, I started to think, were what kept me from being popular with boys. This trend of thought made me at times fantasize over being able to see without wearing glasses. I then could see every male on a street corner waving and whistling at me as I drove by. Coming back into the real world, I decided, "My glasses will have to go!" I had heard about contact lenses but had never known anyone who wore them. Blind, in both sight and knowledge, I decided to be fitted with contacts.

The first contact lenses were made of glass that was ground in Germany. They were torturous objects that only the silliest of sillies would endure. Since I was a first-class silly, I was game to endure their pain. "Anything for beauty" was my philosophy.

My actions were egged on by an incident that took place in Bessemer City during the spring holidays of 1938. My hometown girl-friends had raved about a new boy, Jimmy Ritter, who had come to town to work. While I was in a drug store with a girlfriend, she said, "There's Jimmy. Let me introduce him to you." I quickly snatched off my glasses and hid them in my pocket for the introduction. As the introductions were taking place, the wife of the pharmacist who owned the drug store walked by. She stopped and looked at me, and then pointedly asked in her Yankee manner, "Why Lois! You don't have your glasses on. What happened to them?" I did a quick burn of anger as I grinned at her without answering.

I started immediately being fitted with contacts by an eye specialist in Atlanta. I spent numerous hours in his office trying to condition myself to endure the blinding pain of the contacts. The doctor inserted them in my eyes where they would stay until I gave up. I kept looking at the clock trying to make my minutes of endurance last a little longer with each office visit.

Soon I arrived at the stage where he would have me insert them myself. Prior to inserting the large round pieces of glass onto my eyeballs, I had to put pain-killing drops into my eyes. Using a rubber suction cup, it took patience and a steady hand to fill the lens with saline solution and to insert each lens in the exact center of my eyeball without spilling the solution. When I first got my lenses, the sheer novelty of them prompted the girls on my dorm floor to come and watch me put them into my eyes. Skill was needed to insert them without letting a bubble show in the saline solution. After I inserted them, I ran up and down the hall asking, "Do you see a bubble?" It took more than several girls' words to assure me that no bubbles were floating around in my eyes. I kept wondering, "What would Dorothy Parker say about seeing air pockets in a girl's eyes?"

After going through the procedure of inserting the lenses, if I could stand the pain and was able to keep my eyes open and not tear, I could wear them for a limited time or they would injure my sight, as the eye specialist informed me. I did not think I would be worried with wearing contacts too long. I was worried that I would never be able to wear them long enough for dating purposes.

Along with being fitted for contact lenses, I had caught on to the fact that a student studies at college and does not play at studying, as I had done in high school. At that point, I started making merit grades on some subjects. So did my roommate Anita. Together we rejoiced over our new academic standings. It was a glorious feeling I had as the summer drew near in 1938. I was making good grades and was equipped with contact lenses; I'd traded the Dodge sedan for a pastel yellow Pontiac phaeton convertible and I had a mink coat. Best of all, I was said to have a "knockout figure." I secretly thought, "Oh, happy, lucky me!"

Silently, I joyously announced, "Look out world...Here comes Lossie." No sooner had I started out to dazzle the world, especially the males, when the auto accident did me in. I was knocked into another world, and when I returned, I was never physically the same. The steps I took that day to dazzle were my last. I would never walk again.

But it was the same ole me under those broken bones and bandages. I was still the same flighty, fun-loving girl who would keep on seeing the world through rosy lenses, even if I were a crippled invalid. My accident did not cripple me on the inside. I still had the same personality, the same zest for life. I just could no longer walk.

The last time I did walk was on May 25, 1938. That day, the sun was as dazzling as I hoped I looked wearing my new contact lenses. Anita Howard, Sarah Beatty, and I were in happy spirits because we were getting to do what the other girls wished they could do: go swimming and with boys. As a teenager full of energy and vitality, May 25th for me was like my other days, full of sunshine and happiness. I never dreamed my life could be otherwise. But before the day was over, my life took a drastic change, turning me from a vivacious teenager into a helpless invalid.

So we could ride in a car that afternoon with boys from Georgia Tech, we three girls went by the Dean's office to sign out and to leave the names of the boys. (This was routine now with Anita and me since our freshman year, when the assistant Dean made a visit to our room to point out this regulation.) Our Dean was an elderly woman and was the personification of a Southern Lady. Signing out with her always gave me a guilty feeling because there usually was a hidden factor under my signature that I did not wish to disclose to her. This time was no exception.

Those were the days when blind dates for college girls were about the only chance we had to meet boys. The Dean, who grew up in a Victorian atmosphere, was incapable of comprehending the idea that a young "lady" would date a boy whom she had never met. Both of those dates for Anita and me were blind ones, a fact we did not disclose.

Sarah Beatty, who was scheduled to graduate with my sister on June 7th in ASC's Class of '38, had her father's car to use during graduation. In it we three girls and three Georgia Tech boys took off for an afternoon of fun. Fun for me did not include swimming. Instead I sat by the pool while the others swam. I was wearing my contact lenses publicly for the second time and although they had already started to hurt, I preferred wearing them to swimming. Taking them out and putting them in again was too involved. I cannot remember many incidents about the afternoon except I can recall how I hoped I looked glamorous wearing my German-imported visual aides. The saline solution that filled the round discs made my eyes look bigger, which I prayed was sexy instead of spooky.

Returning to Decatur from the pool near Stone Mountain, Sarah Beatty's date drove her car with her sitting beside him straddling the gears. Anita's date sat beside her. My date sat between Anita and me on the back seat. The last thing I remember about that afternoon was leaning over to tie my saddle oxfords.

For forty years, I never knew the details concerning the wreck itself. I kept it a closed book in the back of my mind. I never asked what took place and no one ever told me. Anyone who

has survived a traumatic experience will understand the terrified reluctance a person feels, wanting to avoid reliving it again
in words. Now that four decades have passed, I am curious
about what did take place, but Mama is gone. I will never know
the total anguish she suffered.

In these forty years I have learned to cope with my handicap. I now keenly want to know just what did take place on
that spring day in '38. The first person I asked was my sister
but her reaction to my questions did not enlighten me. When
my accident took place, Beatrice could not be reached because
she had left Agnes Scott for an early dinner date. I had already
been taken to the emergency room at Emory Hospital by the
time my sister received word of my serious accident, and was
rushed to the emergency room to be with me until my mother
could arrive from North Carolina. I had to prod Bea to get her
to describe how I looked when she first saw my broken body
in the emergency room. The only answer she has ever given me
was to break into sobs while covering her eyes as though to blot
out the picture in her memory as she cried, "You looked awful.
I do not want to ever talk about it again!" And she never has.

Recently, Anita made a visit to see me. When she made plans
for her visit, I thought, "Here is my chance to find out what
really happened because Anita was there!" I was right. Anita remembered our accident vividly and, from the way she told me,
I knew it was not her first time to describe the events.

"That wreck is something I would like to forget but never
will," she said. "In my mind I can see it as clearly as the afternoon it took place. I still have visions of that highway truck
coming down the road. I knew it was supposed to stop, but it
didn't. It just kept coming our way."

Pushing her feet hard against the floor as she re-lived the accident, she recalled, "I braced myself for the crash I knew was
coming." Summing up the cause of the wreck, she said, "The
brakes on the truck failed, and it hit at a right angle into the

front side of our car. After that first impact," she continued, "the two vehicles slammed together like an accordion closing."

She told me the car door where I sat flew open in the initial crash. I received my serious injuries, Anita pointed out, when the truck for the second time smashed into the side of the car where I was bent over tying my saddle oxford.

"The back end of the truck bed came through the opened door and struck you across your back." She added, "The crash left you dangling from the bed of the truck with your face covered in blood." Anita shuddered as she revealed how I looked. "You made a frightful picture!" Even now I have no idea how it happened, but the skin on my forehead peeled back to expose the skull bone. I can well imagine I did make a frightening sight! One thing I did overhear while I was in the hospital was about my saddle oxfords. They stayed where my feet had left them on the car floor.

The accident took place on Covington Road at 5:15 pm. Anita said the first car that came along following the wreck stopped to gape at the gruesome sight of my broken and bleeding body. "I asked the driver to take you to the hospital," Anita recalled. As she told me this I started thinking about how my accident paralleled that of my father. Like me, life was going beautifully for him, he was the only one seriously injured when the boiler explosion took place, and no ambulance service was available to rush him to a hospital.

Thankfully the owner of the car that Anita asked to carry me to Emory Hospital was willing to have his vehicle commandeered for emergency service. "We laid you across the laps of two boys sitting on the back seat," Anita continued. As she told me this, the thought occurred to me that these strangers took me into their car, a bleeding, mangled, and dying teenager and sped me on my way in a mercy mission, and I have never learned the names of my Good Samaritans.

Anita continued, "As other cars stopped, we loaded the oth-

ers who were injured into them and sent them to Emory."
Sarah Beatty who was taken in the second car-ambulance run,
suffered broken ribs. "The boy that was my date," Anita commented in her flat south Georgia accent, "had the front door
handle broken off in his right arm."

Anita told me how she got to the hospital. "After you three
who had been injured had been taken to the hospital, I asked
the driver of another car to take me to Emory." Anita's stay
in the hospital did not last long. She was in and then found
herself practically thrown out. She described her brief hospital stay. "The emergency room supervisor let me go inside the
emergency room. I looked at you and went into hysterics. You
looked terrible! You were lying there, dying, I thought, and I
could not tell one thing was being done to help you."

Already unnerved by the accident, Anita said seeing her
roommate of two years lying there injured with nothing, she
could see, being done for me, was more than her emotions
could stand. She repeated, "I thought the hospital was just letting you lie there and die without even trying to do a thing to
save your life."

Anita would not quiet down, so she was asked to leave. "I
realize now the hospital was doing all it could for you," Anita
said with the understanding that comes with age. "But at the
time, I was so upset that I did not grasp the meaning of the
shock condition your body was in." That state of shock was
the reason that very little could be done for me; when I arrived
at the emergency room, my blood pressure registered zero and
remained in that state longer than anyone else's who had ever
survived, according to the hospital record.

After Beatrice arrived at the hospital, she almost matched
Anita in hysterics before the night was over. Anita, who had
been taken to a friend's house to sleep, awakened and thought
about my contact lenses. She got in touch with Bea at the hospital and found out they were still in my eyes. Together they

begged to have them removed. Beatrice, who had never mentioned any details of my accident, recently told me that, in spite
of the reasons the doctors gave, she, like Anita, wanted my
glass discs removed from my eyeballs.

"Although the doctors did not give us any indication that you
could survive your injuries, I still wanted to have your contacts
removed," my sister told me.

While Beatrice and Anita were battling with the medical authorities to remove my contact lenses, back at my home, my
mother and Central, the telephone operator, received the message of my critical accident at the same time. Today's gener-
ations will never know what an important role the Ole Time
"Central" once played in our lives. Computers and dialing
phones will never find a place in my heart like Central did.

Always a woman and, in small towns, usually a friend, she was
the source of all community news. In addition, hearing what
was going on straight "from the horse's mouth," she served as
general secretary of all the phone company's local customers.
She took and delivered messages.

When the call concerning my accident came in from Atlanta to my mother, Mama and Central heard the disheartening
news together. After Mama's call from Atlanta was completed,
Central came on the line to try to console her. Central at that
hour was Mrs. W.A. Lindsay, a neighbor and close friend. Mama
told Central, "Elta, Lossie is dying and time is against my being
with her." She knew the only train to Atlanta was an 11 p.m.
one, which she feared would not get her to the hospital in time
for her to be with me in my last moments. Mrs. Lindsay told
her, "Don't worry, Anne, you get your things ready and I'll find
someone to drive you to Atlanta."

Mrs. Lindsay wisely contacted Arnold Kincaid, who owned a
textile machine shop in Bessemer City. According to the consensus of the local populace, he was the best person to make
this mercy run since he knew the roads, having traveled them

on business trips, and he was considered the fastest and best driver in town. With the help of friends who quickly gathered, Mama had her things ready when Mr. Kincaid arrived to drive her on their fast trip to Atlanta. My mother left for Atlanta knowing I was still alive but not knowing what my condition would be when she arrived at the hospital. The prayers of her family and friends rode with her as she and Mr. Kincaid sped to Georgia with no holds barred.

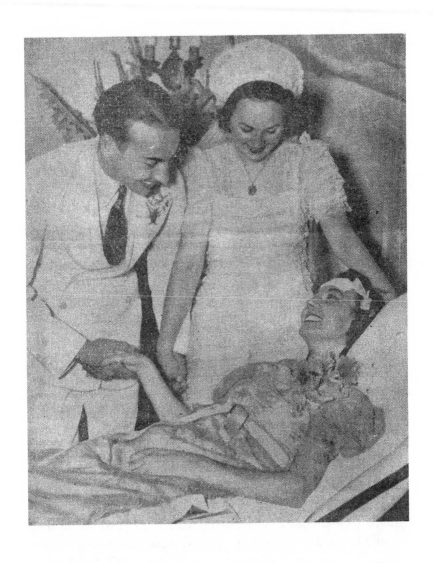

Lois photographed for *Atlanta Journal Constitution* with newlyweds Beatrice and Carl Howard

5

Chapter Five

My mother arrived at the hospital at 1:30 a.m. on Thursday, May 26, 1938. By the time she reached my bedside, the spirit of life in me was at such a low ebb that all the doctors had done for me was slit my ankles to give me glucose and blood transfusions. No attempts had been made to clean off the blood and grime, set my broken bones, sew up my torn flesh or remove my contacts from my eyes. On finding out my contacts were still in my eyes, my mother joined Anita and Beatrice insisting that they be removed. By removing them, my mother thought it would give a gleam of hope that I might survive instead of die.

Between Anita's adamant urgings, my sister's tears, and my mother's hurt looks, they called out the Atlanta specialist who had fitted them in the early hours of the 26th to remove them. They had stayed in my eyes for twelve hours. The longest I had ever worn them was two hours. I feel I owe my eyesight now to female hysterics. With no registering of my blood pressure coupled with the lenses inserted over a lengthy period, I feel certain I would have lost my vision if they had not been removed when they were. Since my accident, I have never worn my contact lenses again.

They have been worn once since May of 1938 when I loaned them to a friend, Boyce Rhyne, who wanted to see if they could be used while swimming. One time wearing them must have been enough for him because he never asked to borrow them again.

After my lenses were removed and the medical specialists who attended me were able to examine me, they had nothing but disheartening things to tell my family. They pointed out that since I had gone such a lengthy period with no blood pressure, my brain did not get sufficient blood, and they surmised I would be a vegetable for the rest of my life. In addition to being a vegetable, I would be a quadriplegic, paralyzed from the neck down because two vertebrae in the 4th and 5th dorsal had been mashed and pushed out of line, severing my spinal cord. Other injuries included a brain concussion and three or four breaks in my left arm. I was in a sorry condition and I looked sorry, too, with half my forehead's skin peeled back to reveal bare skull. Knowing all this, I do not see how my family had the heart to want me to survive enough to even pray for my recovery. But pray they did.

As my mother and sister looked at me lying there, for all they knew I was already a "vegetable." With my scalp denuded of skin, I can imagine they had the fleeting thoughts that if my brains should come spilling out, would they look like brains or vegetable soup? I had suffered a blow across one of my eyes which left it discolored. Both eyes were swollen shut and several of my teeth had broken off. My condition was worse than sorry. It made me look scary!

My broken body and teeth and bare scalp were lying there in the hospital bed but my spirit from late Wednesday to Sunday afternoon was elsewhere. People around my physical body were suffering for my sake, but at the time I was not in their world.

I was in a beautiful world of my own. My world was a twilight zone. I don't know if angels sang but music was there, beauty was there, and flowers were everywhere. But the greatest feeling that consumed me was a feeling of peace and contentment. In that blissful state, I could feel the pressure of people, my mother, my sister, trying to take me out of my spiritual state. I protested. This place was mine! I did not want to leave it. I felt as though I was being taken out of paradise against my will.

While I was still protesting, all at once my mother's face appeared before me. She kissed me. My first words to her after my accident were, "That is a Judas kiss." Being pulled from my peaceful place, did I feel that the one person closest to me had betrayed me? I have often pondered, what made me make that statement? In the process of leaving my beautiful place, I kept shouting, "I will not. I will not!"

My sister told me I had been at my lowest point of survival and doctors had asked help from both her and my mother to get me to take some medicine. In my lifeless state, I had struggled and protested. Were my protests over taking the medicine or over leaving my peaceful state? Only God knows.

As I emerged from my other world, I was amazed to see my friends from home surrounding me. Using my right hand, my good one, I pried open my less black and swollen eye to look. Standing around my bed were Wissie Gray, Caroline Mauney, Mary Alice Horsley, Bill Smith, Bill Lindsay, along with Anita, Aunt Pearl and Uncle John Doyle, Aunt Essie and Uncle John Hunter Phifer and my cousins Jean and Helen Phifer, Aunt Alda, Uncle Robert Sexton, Aunt Ede and Uncle Joe Rothman. Friends and relatives were all over the place and I could not comprehend the situation.

Where had they come from and why? It was as though someone had slid a different slide into my projector. In time I grasped the fact that the slide I was seeing from my hospital bed was out of focus. Something was not right. What had happened to me to bring friends and relatives from far distances to smile at me? What was so bad about my injuries that people would drive to Atlanta and back, to Bessemer City and other places, in the same day just to stand over my bed for a few minutes?

While having happy feelings over seeing loved ones, I had silent thoughts that were frightening. Eventually, something inside made me aware that there was something terribly wrong with me. In time my mind signaled to me the fact that I could not move my legs. I knew I would never be able to move again. The realization that I was paralyzed was such a shattering shock that I did not want to talk about it to anyone.

Like a kid knowing the truth about Santa Claus, I kept my discovery of my physical condition to myself. I began living in a make believe world in which everything would be better tomorrow. My beliefs that tomorrow would be better served as my crutch for the rest of my life.

At the age of eighteen, it was not make believe but real. I still wanted life to be beautiful for me and I wanted to be beautiful with it. Bill Smith, the red headed Yankee who had moved to my hometown, and whom I dated in high school, claims the first words he heard me utter on his first visit to the hospital were, "Where's the mirror?" Days passed into weeks before anyone had the heart to hand me a mirror. By the time I was handed a mirror, my physical condition, along with my looks had improved -- but they both could still be termed as sorry spectacles.

While I never discussed my condition with my doctors, my mother did. The most comforting aspect they could give her was that I would probably die within the year or, at the longest, in two years. And if I did live longer than that, they reasoned, I would never be able to care for myself in any way.

No one could give a definite prediction about my outcome, because up until that time, people in my physical condition died from either pneumonia or from kidney infection. But for me, there was a new "wonder" drug, sulfa, that had just started to be used. A glucose specialist from England happened to be at Emory when I was admitted as an emergency patient. With her knowledge and doses of sulfa, I pulled through. When first used, sulfa must have been thought to destroy red blood cells because every few days, nurses would remove my colored nail polish, and check to see if my nails had a grayish look. But my nails kept their normal color and I have kept taking sulfa. For the past forty years it still has positive results.

Everything my doctors did for me helped preserve my life. They kept me alive but there was no prescription available for them to predict how I could live a meaningful life. Medical professionals could tell my mother what my problems likely would be, but they had no precedents to indicate what I could achieve. My broken body was just like Humpty Dumpty. Once broken, none of the kings of the medical world "could put me back together again." My injuries were patched up, but the cracks were still there and I would never be the same again. It would have been the end for me if I had copped-out on my handicaps. To survive, I learned with time to cope with my handicaps by living each day to the fullest, with the hope that tomorrow would be better.

This eternal grasping for better tomorrows has been my sustaining force through the years. As I waited in my make-believe world at Emory Hospital, I did not fully understand the serious extent of my handicaps for my future. I was kept too busy by the presence of my doctors and nurses to have time to think. My day and night nurses constantly worked with me during their 12-hour shifts. I was turned on the hour to prevent pressure sores, and I was "watered" every hour to keep my kidneys and bladder functioning. Pneumonia developed and I had to have my lungs aspirated twice to draw off fluids. I also underwent major surgery to my spinal column and to my bladder. My broken ribs repaired themselves.

Because of the length of time I stayed in a state of shock with zero blood pressure readings, the torn flesh on my forehead was never sewn nor the broken bones in my left arm set. A heavy cast was placed on my arm and sores developed under it from the dirt left from the wreck. The sores did not hurt under my cast but they itched. An Atlanta woman, who had become interested in me after reading about my accident in the paper, brought me a stay from one of her corsets to use to scratch my "itches" by running it under the cast. Like that woman, several Atlanta people I had never known visited me frequently in the hospital, their concern growing into lasting friendship.

Each day I dreaded having the strips of adhesive pulled off my exposed scalp and having my body turned. I felt like crying when a doctor came to my bedside daily to pull off the adhesive from my tender scalp to clean it before placing fresh adhesive on my injured forehead in hopes it would close the wide gap of open skull.

Because of the heavy cast on my arm, it took several people to turn me. Even with all the helping hands, I suffered excruciating pain each time I was moved.

Along with my heavy schedule of being nursed and cared for, I had a steady stream of visitors. All this helped to push to the unthinking part of my mind the pathetic shape I was in. I looked forward to seeing everyone, especially the interns. I thought they were so handsome, and fell in love with all of them. Although the smoke from their cigarettes would lay me low because of the fluid in my lungs, it always thrilled me when interns came into my room to sneak a smoke.

I have decided now that some of the interns' and doctors' numerous visits were not necessary, as when they came into my room frequently to examine the exact point where my paralysis started. Although I was small boned and just a slip of a girl, I had bosoms that looked like over sized ice cream cones turned upside down. These bosoms received considerable attention during medical evaluation because the point of my "not feeling" was right at the nipple area of my bosoms. Every doctor or intern who came near me would use a sharp pointed object to prick my bosoms after telling me to let them know when the place they pricked did not have a feeling sensation. Each time that I was pricked with a sharp object, I silently prayed, while holding my breath, I could say I felt the prick as it continued down my bosom and that my paralysis had gone away. Sadly, I could see with the ones examining me the point of not feeling never changed. It always stayed in the same location -- but with each new prick I experienced a surge of hopeful anticipation that a miracle would happen. These prick examinations could have been done to my back as well as to my bosom, but my back was never used once as a pricking ground.

My days of living in the present came to a standstill when the time came that the future had to be dealt with, not entirely for me, but for my sister. While I spent my time in college trying to pass my scholastic courses, Beatrice had settled on a course of matrimony. At the time of my accident, she had already announced her engagement to Carl Wiley Howard, who was no relation to my roommate, Anita, but, like Anita, was from Georgia. Bea had bought her wedding dress and, with Carl, had set their wedding date for June, following her graduation at Scott on June 7, 1938, and Carl's at Emory University on June 8, 1938.

My being hospitalized for an indefinite period created a problem for Cupid. But not for my aunts.

Guiding Beatrice in her decisions, Mama and her sisters decided that the wedding would go on as planned, not in June but in July, and not in Bessemer City but in Atlanta. Working on the premise that after their marriage, Bea and Carl would want to live near Emory University where Carl had enrolled in the School of Law, the planners asked, "Why not buy a house near Emory?" Buying a house solved many problems. Mama and the various friends and relatives who came to visit me while I was hospitalized stayed in the house during their visits. The Howard-Sexton wedding, reduced from a large affair to a small informal event, was now set to take place in the house so that I could attend the ceremony.

By the time of my sister's new wedding date, July 9, 1938,

things were looking up for me. My looks were back to normal. The heavy cast had been removed from my left arm, even though doctors had told my mother it was paralyzed when she first arrived at the hospital. I could not use it, but it was not paralyzed. Nor was I a quadriplegic or a vegetable -- so my future was not quite as dire as first predicted. I was a paraplegic, which is bad enough, but far from being either of those.

My doctors agreed I was able to be a member of the wedding party. Attending my sister's wedding would mark my first time venturing out of Emory Hospital as an invalid. Trying to bolster my spirit and nerve for this new experience, my family, nurses, and hospital staff hovered around my bed getting me ready for the affair. Mama bought me a pastel pink lace housecoat and Beatrice brought me my first orchid. To "pretty me up," my nurse, Mrs. Ballard, put a pink ribbon in my hair, pink nail polish on my finger and toe nails, and a small bandage instead of adhesive over my scalp injury.

All dressed for my first outing, I was rolled from my room on my hospital bed to a waiting ambulance by Rufus, the orderly on my floor. During my stay at Emory, Rufus always treated me like a baby when he had to handle the heavy cast on my left arm for my hourly turn. As Rufus made his way down the hospital corridor with me, he stopped at opened doors of different rooms to let the other patients see me dressed for the wedding. I had been at the hospital long enough for other patients to be familiar with my condition and progress. In a sense, I held star-status among the patients and nurses because of the outward attitude I had displayed accepting my crippling injuries. I admit it was no occasion for flattery to be held up as an example to other patients when they were down in the dumps, in that my situation was worse than theirs. But that was the position I found myself in.

Along with my happy outlook on life, I had too much pride to cry on other people's shoulders. I could live with my infirmities but could not live with the thoughts that others pitied and tolerated me. This aspect of my personality prevented me from ever showing outward bitterness. I was like an alcoholic who knows he is a drunkard but will not admit it. I knew I was a cripple but I did not want to talk or think about it. I never used the term "paraplegic" at first because when I became one, I did not know there was such a word: even less, how to spell it. Like the public, I became more familiar with the term during the Vietnam War.

As Rufus pushed my bed along the hospital corridor, I did not feel like a cripple. I felt like Cinderella dressed in my new finery, instead of gown and bed jacket. I was in a happy mood as different ones waved me off, but as soon as the ambulance headed toward the wedding, I started having a feeling of apprehension at the thought that this would be my first time after my accident to be with a large nvgroup of people. I started worrying what their reaction would be to me. Would they look at me with pity or would they act blase? As I was carried into the house on the ambulance cot, I wished I were back in the haven of the hospital where staff members knew me and accepted my condition.

These fears were forgotten as soon as my ambulance cot was placed inside the living room, where an improvised altar had been erected in front of the mantel. Instead of a strained occasion of people standing back, and not knowing what to say to me, everyone crowded around me, making the wedding seem like a homecoming event. I was full of talk and smiles as loved ones gathered around my cot. I was happy to be a part of the festivities as they took place instead of hearing about them after they were over, like I had to do when Beatrice graduated from Scott. As I chatted and laughed with the wedding guests, I was filled with complete euphoria.

The joyous sparkle of my smiles came to an abrupt end when the solemnity of the occasion struck me. It had struck my sister first. Soon after my arrival, Bea's eyes and nose became rosy red from the shower of tears she shed when she realized the significance of her marriage and how it would affect her family. She knew that by leaving home she would cause the first break in our all-female household. For years it had been Mama, Bea, and me standing together to meet life. Now that I could no longer stand, Bea felt she was deserting me, and my sister sobbed. Feelings of guilt plagued her that she was not doing right by me. I would soon be leaving the hospital to return home, where she knew her "little sister" would need her "big sister" to make adjustments for her altered life. As Bea had always been around to see after me, she realized not being there would create a keen void in my feelings of security.

Seeing my sister's tears at this moment that should have been one of the happiest of her life, I too was filled with guilt. I kept thinking, "Maybe I should not have come." The thought struck me that my presence in my crippled condition was too sad a spectacle to add any happiness. At that moment, the deepest depression I had experienced since my accident dissipated my previous joy. Both the present and the future became ominous times for me. Despite these sad thoughts, I was able to keep tears from rolling down my face, although I could not remove the unhappy look from my frozen smile.

Although Bea, Mama and I did get our emotions under control, I feared our sadness had permeated the wedding. I later wondered if the officiating minister became confused over whether he was conducting a wedding or a funeral. After the ceremonies, our good spirits returned. My new brother-in-law looked so radiant with happiness that his smile was contagious. An Atlanta newspaper photographer took pictures -- the bridegroom, bride, and then me, which were carried by the wire services. As the newly married couple stood over my ambulance cot to pose with me for one of the pictures, we looked a joyous threesome. Our expressions were now alive with a lighthearted gaiety, and the affair become renewed with a cheerful and merry atmosphere.

At the time I was lying there on the ambulance cot filled with sadness, if I could have only seen into the future, then the prospects would not have seemed so desolate. Little did I dream as I held back sobs over losing my only sister, that one day she, her husband, their children and bird dogs would live with Mama and me, and that before many years passed, the Howards would be the family that lived next door!

But things never stay the same. When the 1938-39 term started at Agnes Scott, Bea and Sarah Beatty had graduated, and the dorm room that Anita and I had reserved for the term was empty. I became a college drop-out and Anita, crushed over the accident, transferred to the University of Georgia at Athens. My closest ties to Scott were gone.

Lois at picnic with friends in her sling chair

6

Chapter Six

After my sister's wedding, my next time to leave from the hospital was on July 14, 1938. Bessemer City had no ambulance so Mama's friend, Frank Sisk, owner of Sisk Funeral Home, sent a hearse to Atlanta from Bessemer City to take me home, along with my teenage cousin, Marie Phifer. Mrs. Wilmarth, one of my Atlanta nurses, accompanied me to Bessemer City where she nursed me for the remainder of the summer months. How I hated to leave Emory Hospital. It had become my home and its staff a part of my family.

I left the hospital in tears when the time came to carry me out on the ambulance cot. The hospital personnel who had taken care of me almost matched me in my sadness as they came to see me homeward bound. Like me, they felt apprehensions about my immediate future. I knew I would be facing a new way of life, but they felt I was facing an early death. With so many things wrong with me, doctors were still predicting to my family that death for me was imminent. They thought my death would be a blessing but one deeply marked by disconsolate sorrow.

As the hearse pulled away from Emory Hospital, my thoughts were concerned not with death but with facing the outside world and living in it as a cripple. I felt a mixture of fear and eagerness knowing I was going home. Unfortunately I was lying on the cot in such a position that I could not cast a final look at Emory, a place to which I had become attached but would never see again.

I could see the inside of the hearse, and loaded as it was with my things, it looked more like a moving van than a conveyance for the ill or dead. Mrs. Wilmarth had packed potted plants, goldfish, and gifts wherever there was a space she could place them.

Enroute to North Carolina, while passing through South Carolina, we stopped in a small town for lunch at a drive-in. Mama sat up front with the driver. Mrs. Wilmarth and cousin Marie were in the back with me. A waiter took our curb-side orders from the front seat and then Marie called out her order from the back. The waiter nearly fainted thinking he was hearing from the dead.

Shoppers, seeing a hearse parked at a curb-side drive-in, came up to peer inside our windows. Seeing me lying there smiling instead of dead sent them quickly away. I peered back at them with matching interest as I munched on a hot dog with onions. I enjoyed watching people walking up and down the street almost as much as I enjoyed my hot dog. Riding inside the hearse in the July heat, with only a small fan running, I realized it was not adequate to cool its glassed-in closeness. The nearer we came to home, the more anxious I became to get there.

When we reached Kings Mountain, only seven miles from Bessemer City, I anxiously looked out the window, hoping to hurry up getting home. When the hearse pulled into our drive and the attendants carried me inside, the coolness of its interior greeted me. I knew then that home was a good place to be. With the house filled with cut flowers and friends, memories of the tears I had shed leaving the hospital were forgotten, as were my fears of entering the outside world. My life, though pathetically altered, continued to be as it had been before: filled with love and laughter. In addition to my own eagerness to live each day to its fullest, my family and friends rallied to boost my spirits as they helped me live with my handicaps.

In many ways, I was fortunate that my accident happened in the late 1930's. The impoverishments of the Great Depression had touched almost everyone and people still looked to one another for their needs. Going out of the 1930's into the '40's was indeed a good time to be handicapped because people sincerely cared. In the back of my mind, I recalled how families and the public had treated imperfect persons while I was growing up; I had visions of cripples and the mentally impaired being shoved away in a back room while families pretended they were not really there. When I arrived home as an invalid, no one shoved me into a back room to hide me from sight. Instead, I soon became a community rehabilitation project, cared for by the young and old.

My hometown friends were united in their attempts to make my miseries go away. At that time, just as young people danced the Big Apple to juke box music as though they, too, were dancing away miseries of their own, across the ocean World War II was brewing. While my physical body was changed, people seemed to clutch to one another to live, laugh and cry. As a crippled teenager, I was included in their activities and my handicaps quietly merged with other people's problems, problems they quietly assumed without making a todo. Together, we became one big family, and turned my adjustment to a restricted life into a happy family affair.

In those days, most young people still manufactured their entertainment at home. They pursued their fun in groups, and having a good time required creative resources. In my role as a cause celebre, I gave my family and friends a focus for creating our homespun pleasures.

People forty years ago seemed more willing to share -- they shared cars for double and triple dates. As the only paraplegic in the area, people shared me, which I must confess, I enjoyed. This was my reality as I arrived home on July 14, 1938. Instead of being placed in a back room, I was accepted as one of the crowd.

My homecoming called for a celebration, so my next door neighbor Dora Sherman thought. She arranged for an open

house at my home the day after I returned to Bessemer City
from Emory Hospital. The hearse crew returned to carry
me downstairs from my upstairs bedroom. Once more I was
dressed in my pink lace housecoat to lie on an ambulance cot
for a social affair. Friends lined up to file by my cot to shake my
good hand and tell me how happy they were that I had pulled
through and was back home. Even though I had come back to
my hometown a helpless invalid, they wanted me to know how
good it was to have me back with them. I should have felt sad
over being there in such a broken physical condition, but my
happiness at being home and back in the family fold kept me
from realizing the pathos of the occasion.

It is remembering such times as these that I now look back
and wonder, "How could I have felt so complacent over my
bleak fate?" Among the strong contributing factors was the
fact that even during the depression, Southerners never gave
up their hospitality. My returning home from the hospital and
the presence of an out of state nurse called for Southern cour-
tesies.

Welcome mats were put out for me and my nurse, and people took turns having all of us as dinner guests. This included
whatever family members or friends were at the time sleeping
at our house. If the hostess happened to be of the Presbyterian
faith, thir minister was also included, thus killing two birds with
one stone. It was as though I was an engaged girl or a debu-
tante, as on these occasions people brought out their best serving ware along with crispy linen napkins, always home baked
breads, fresh vegetables in season and home-churned peach or
strawberry ice cream. With all of this being done for me, what
could have been finer than convalescing in "Ka-lie-nah" in the
Summer of '38?

It soon turned out that my struggle to learn how to live with
my handicaps could be too much of a good thing. Just how the
nurses did everything for me in the hospital, now at home, my

mother, friends, and registered nurse continued to do everything for me. Treated like a helpless invalid, I became one. My
first winter of paraplegia was spent living the life of a totally
helpless cripple. I was carried everywhere I went, and spent
most of my days lying on my bed and letting others take care
of me or keep me entertained. I did not even put on my own
lipstick or comb my hair. I barely moved a muscle except to
open and close my eyes.

In recent years I have asked myself where was my pride?
What had happened to turn me into a parasite that existed by
sapping the energies of others? I had always been more of an
independent thinker than a follower. Recalling my first year of
being an invalid, I realized it was my physical weakness more
than my emotional state which kept me from rehabilitating
myself.

Arriving home six weeks after suffering the vast physical
damages that were predicted to shorten my life expectancy, I
did not have the stamina to even attempt to grab the world by
the tail. Taking the easy way out, I became content to hold onto
my mother's apron strings.

I was fortunate to have the mother I did. Now that her "baby"
was back home, she did her best to make our home atmosphere
as pleasant and convenient for me as she could. Our house's
architectural design was such that it had all upstairs bedrooms.
The day I was carried into the house after my trip home from
Emory, I was placed in my bedroom on one of my twin beds.
I As my involved schedule progressed smoothly, I considered
myself all set up, with Mrs. Wilmarth sharing the other twin
bed. When she left to return to Atlanta that fall, Mama bought
a hospital bed and placed it on the downstairs sun porch, which
had an outside entrance and was located near the kitchen, the
hub of our household activities. When it came time for me to
be moved, I rebelled. My twin bed suited me, but it did not
suit those who had to run up and down stairs to wait on me. I

balked but I was moved.

Once, while I was out one afternoon, Mama moved my vanity dresser, chest of drawers, and bureau from my bedroom to the sun porch and placed them there with my hospital bed. When I returned home and saw what had been done, I cried. I wanted my bedroom to stay the same. That was my room, and it was all too much to make my situation seem so final. Just like when I left the hospital, I cried and wanted to stay in my old room.

It is still hard for me to make a change, and making major changes always depresses me. It is still hard for me to leave one thing that I have become used to and exchange it for something new. Changes mean readjustments and it is harder for handicapped people to adjust.

Mama did one thing I did not fuss about when she gave free room and board in our garage apartment to a most attractive bachelor ministerial student who served our church for the '38 summer months. The only thing she wanted in return was for Sam Milton to help out driving me places. My mother could not drive nor lift and carry me when I had occasions to leave the house. When the ambulance drove into our driveway that hot day in July, there was Sam Milton ready to carry me. Having Sam as a friend made the beginning of my life as a cripple an easy transition. "Preacher Sam," I called him, and I'll always love him for what he did for me when I first became an invalid. Good looking, witty, and termed a "woman killer," he found that girls flocked around him. Since he was with me, the girls flocked to our house, and where the girls are gathered, so are the boys. The rest of the Summer of '38, the Sextons were holding Open House day and night for the younger set with the ministerial student as the star attraction.

Sam, wherever you are, I will never forget you. You were the first of many males to carry me cuddled in your arms. Not with romantic intentions, but as a Boy Scout Good Deed. At this point in my life, male scouts were good things to have around --

Johnny Crasney, Willie Moore, Pinckney Stowe, Charles Isbill, Buddy Mauney, Billy Gamble, Jimmy Ritter, Jerry Wyatt and a troop of others. I will always love every one of them! Without any equivocation, I declare that Boys are A Girl's Best Friends. How could a helpless girl have lived without the husky males who came to her rescue and placed her into the field of action? That's the way I feel about the young men who helped me cope with my handicaps.

My spineless, weak, and helpless state must have appealed to their strong male instinct. Having gone through girlhood as an unpopular wren, I was happy to be carried along my merry way by a number of young men willing to devote their time and attention to me. I began to think my accident had served as a molting agent and I was now clothed in colorful plumage. In my invalid condition, I eagerly (and with a good bit of audacity) imposed on masculine strength as I adjusted to my new way of life. I have never been the cause of any heartache among the male sex, but I know I must have been responsible for many a back ache!

Now Johnny Crasney, he was a different kind of Scout. A Jewish refugee from Germany in 1938, Johnny rented a bedroom from my Aunt Alda at the Phifer home, so he could work in the local textile mills owned by Jewish families. Childless "Ont Olda," as Johnny called my aunt, took him to her bosom like the orphan in a strange country he was. He became a member of our family.

Coming from a wealthy and educated class, Johnny, who had lived a colorful life, did not enter into the marathon race of carrying me in his arms, but his visits and friendship did help push away boredom during those first long, winter months when a good many of my friends had returned to college.

After Sam Milton left that summer to enter a seminary, I never saw him again. While he was with us, his ambition was to be called to a Presbyterian Church in Florida where he could fish and play golf the year 'round. I often wondered if he got his wish.

In the spring of 1939, Mama took in her next free boarders: Jimmy Ritter and Jerry Wyatt. Jimmy had come to town while I was in college to work in the offices of the textile chain owned by Jerry's family. Uncle Mike Reeves, Jerry's bachelor uncle and chairman of the board of directors, sent his nephew to Bessemer City to learn textiles from the bottom up. I don't know if Jerry learned much about textiles while a "learner" at Osage Mill, but he did learn how to have a good time during his stay in Bessemer City.

Jimmy and Jerry attracted the girls as much as Sam Milton had. While Sam sported a Model A Ford convertible, Jerry and Jimmy owned a Chevrolet convertible plus a motorcycle, the only ones in our crowd with a bike. When they were not buzzing around dazzling the girls in their convertible, they boomed around town on their motorcycle. As with Sam, the girls flocked around Jimmy and Jerry, and the boys gathered around the girls, and our house continued having Open House day and night during the summer of 1939 and into the summer of 1940.

While Jimmy and Jerry made their home with us, they painted the wood on our brick house, which was no small job since we had over fifty outside windows with window panes.

I don't know how the boys rated "helping out with Lossie," but painting the house turned into a lark for them. Dressed in painter's caps and coveralls, they stood high on their ladders to reach the eaves, and kept saying, "You don't smear it on -- you slap the paint on!" Their peppy slap, slap, slaps keeping time to the music coming over the radio turned them into modern day Tom Sawyers attracting eager helpers.

They did such good work that Mama gave them a bonus by having them drive Mama, Bea, and me on a swing through the Southern states, including a stopover visit in Rodessa, Louisiana, with the Sextons.

For our Southern Adventure, we traveled like sports. Mama had swapped the yellow Pontiac convertible Phaeton for a black 1939 Buick phaeton convertible with red trim and red upholstery, spare tires in the front fenders, and, to give it a touch of class, white sidewall tires.

While we rode the roads in high style, I was carried around on the ground by the boys on a makeshift contraption invented by my carriers. Not having or wanting a wheelchair for traveling and sightseeing, I used a Tote Stool that Jimmy and Jerry designed for me by putting straps onto a folding, backless canvas camp stool. When the riggings on my carrying stool were attached to it, the boys slung the straps over their shoulders after having plumped me down on the stool. I was set for going and they were set for walking. As they walked along, I dangled in between them on the stool with my arms entwined tightly around their necks. This was fun for me. Instead of having to crane my neck to look up to the conversation from my usual low-ground position, there I was on high ground where I could turn my head from side to side to talk to the boys as we "walked" along. It was good to be on the same level again as a normal person walking and talking!

With their inventive equipment for the handicapped, we made a compact threesome along the tourist stops. When our trio covered the Seminole Indian village in Florida, Indian children followed me around giving me the eye as much as the tourists who had paid to eye them.

At resting points, I would sit with my legs crossed to give sitting-up support while my stool and I were grounded, and Indian children gathered closer to look and gape at me, mainly at my forehead scar. After commenting to a Seminole woman about the obvious interest the children had in my scar, the woman, whether teasing or not, told us the children thought I had been branded for doing something bad. If wickedness was the reason for being branded among the Seminoles, with my big "W" must have made me look like a mighty wicked person to the Indian children.

Before we left Silver Springs, Mama insulted one husky male who was dressed with feathers in his hair and wore a skirt of many colors. Looking the Indian over from head to his bare feet, Mama filled with curiosity, finally mustered the nerve to hesitantly ask, "Are you man or woman?" The skirt was the thing that had puzzled Mama. The Indian puffed out his chest in indignation, pounded himself on his breast and roared, "Me man!!"

At times when my bearers stopped for a rest, before they bent to their task of picking me up to resume our "walking," they bravely pounded their chests while exclaiming, "Me man!" And then they briskly trotted me off to another site.

When we crossed the Mississippi to Vicksburg on a ferry, with my two carriers and my camp stool, I did not have to stay put inside the car in the hold. Instead I went out out on deck with the other travelers to watch the "Mighty River Keep on Rollin'." The captain of the boat became friendly with us and let the two boys go inside the pilot house where they blew the ferry boat's whistle and waved to me from their vantage point.

On our tour trip, Jimmy, Jerry, and I were grouped together. Beatrice, now as a married matron, paired with Mama, and the two acted in a more mature manner than we three younger ones.

Being with Jimmy, Jerry, and Sam was like having big brothers while they were with us. They dated other girls and I dated other boys, and our friendship remained on sister and brother levels. If my mother had conducted a nationwide search, she could not have found any more attractive or kinder boys. Sam was like having Clark Gable with Bob Hope's wit as our house guest. My boyfriends usually liked Sam, but they detested Jerry and Jimmy because they felt they were competing with Robert Redford and Burt Reynolds whenever the two "J's" were around.

Jimmy and Jerry knew the way my boyfriends felt, and with devilish delight they would wait until my date and I rode into our driveway; while my date was getting out of the car on his side, they would come racing to my side, open the door and grab me up and run into the house with me, leaving my date fuming mad.

My friendship with Jerry and Jimmy came to an end that fall when they enlisted in the U.S. Navy. They were discharged after World War II, but never returned to Bessemer City. When they left, I kept the stool they had made and used it for different occasions so I could be with the crowd, which meant so much to me. I had not always been included in the crowd growing up as I wanted to be. Being with the ones I liked now gave me a happy feeling. As the baby in our family, I had tagged along with Bea and her crowd, and with Thomas and his crowd, but I was not always welcomed.

I was the lackey for running errands. But I ran them, happy to be with the gang. Even when I was the butt of their jokes, I never felt humiliated. I was too happy being with the older kids to care. Bea did not resent my tagging along as much as Thomas. Many times before my brother died, he would frequently plead, "Mama, don't let Lois follow me!" One of the best friends he had before he died was Rufus Plonk. Like all the other girls, I had a crush on Rufus, who was as indifferent to me as he was good looking. He had a dog named "Dixie" that he would sic on us girls. Shrieking in happy distress, we climbed trees to get out of the reach of Dixie's teeth.

Dixie treed me many times as I chased after Rufus and Dixie chased after me. Now with my new-found status at the center of the crowd, I was happy to climb down from my treed era.

After Sam, Jimmy, and Jerry, we never had any more free boarders. We did have some live-ins, but they were paid help, such as Eurlene. After my accident, we usually looked to the farms for domestic help, where our selections were based more on brawn than any ability to do household chores. Since I weighed less than ninety pounds, picking me up and carrying me around did not require an Atlas. Even my girlfriends could snatch me up to carry me short distances.

Eurlene could handle me like a baby. A comely black female with an Amazon build, she could team up with my registered nurse and together carry me to such places as the dentist's office to have my wreck-broken teeth taken care of. As a live-in maid, she rode a bus each weekend to her home near Lincolnton, North Carolina. Her rooms were in our basement where she had her own bathroom and shower. Her sleeping quarters were located underneath our first floor hall bath. One week night, my mother was awakened by the smell of tobacco smoke.

Since no one in our family smoked, she grew alarmed. Investigating its source led her to the hall bathroom where the odor of smoke was emerging through the heat vents along with strange noises. Excited over the situation in the early hour of the morning, Mama called the police to come and check out what was going on. After two policemen arrived, Mama had them listen through the heat grill located so near the floor that the police had to almost lie down on the bathroom floor to hear.

As they stealthily made their way down the dark basement steps with guns drawn, their actions almost ended in tragedy. Creeping in the dark down the steps in single file, the policeman in front stopped in his place and the policeman behind him didn't, and rammed his gun into the back of the policeman in front, scaring him out of his wits. Later the policeman's tale of the night's event made the incident sound like a Keystone Cops comedy.

The source of the unusual sound turned out to be a male visitor Eurlene was entertaining in her boudoir. The night caller's identity would forever remain a mystery. Where he had come from and how he arrived were unknown since no car was in sight. We never mentioned the incident to Eurlene and she never commented about it to us.

Before the year's end, Eurlene went home for her usual weekend visit. Prior to catching the bus time, she had complained of a stomach ache. After she caught the bus later that day, we never saw her again. Her father called on Sunday to tell us that Eurlene had become a mother. Neither her parents nor my family had noticed the slightest indication that Eurlene was expecting. Mama always blamed that midnight visitor for Eurlene's fate.

Lois, Wissie and her date

7

Chapter Seven

In my last year as a teenager, I acted more like a high school sophomore than the college student I should have been. Frivolous and irresponsible, I thought more about enjoying life than I did about facing the reality of it.

I drifted from day to day letting others worry about my problems until one of my aunts came for a visit. I had been a paraplegic for almost a year when Aunt Pearl Doyle arrived. She found me accepting my situation that I had no choice but to live a doll's life. I had been babied all my life and so it came easy for me to let others do the work for me. The first winter that I lay at home in my hospital bed, Mama and Bea fretted over me, trying to arrive at some course of action that would help me through what they believed would be long, dreary days.

In a state of indecision, they decided that maybe a parrot or a monkey would add zest to my life. I may have appeared to be a simple minded Pollyanna, but I could not agree with them that either a monkey or a parrot would give meaning to my life.

When Aunt Pearl arrived for her visit, she had different ideas for me than a monkey or parrots when she observed me letting others put on my lipstick and comb my hair. To put her ideas into action, she adroitly maneuvered my mother into another room for a conference -- the bathroom in fact -- as it is the only place in our house that afforded privacy. After their confab, they emerged from their headquarters, approached me, and with determination in their voices, gave me some "plain talking."

"Lossie," Aunt Pearl began her pep talk. "Don't you think

it is about time that you started doing things for yourself?"
Pointing to my toothbrush, she said, "Such as brushing your
own teeth." Handing me a tube of lipstick, she added, "And
putting on your lipstick." I was delighted. The thought had
not occurred to me that I could do things for myself. For the
first time I realized that instead of copping out of living, I
could cope with life on my own. When the fact sank in that just
because I was an invalid it did not mean I had to live the life
of one, I started my first "steps" toward rehabilitation. After
they pushed me into action I never stopped, as I threw off the
shackles of helplessness and started a future of taking care of
myself.

Always impulsive, my mind flipped to thinking "First things
first...my looks!" Examining myself in my mirror, I decided the
thing that could give me "oomph" would be a permanent for
my straggly hair. Arrangements were made for a beauty parlor
operator to come to my house to give me a permanent. When
I had my first permanent, the operator used electric rollers to
burn curls into my hair. This one used solutions. I thought
I would drown before my beauty-crew got through tugging
at me to get my head into a position where my hair could be
doused again and again with water. When all the commotion
was over, I was pleased with the new "Me" I saw reflected in
my mirror. The new crinkles in my hair did improve my looks.

After enjoying my new coiffure for a week, with the help of
home folks, we undertook the task of shampooing my hair for
the first time since getting my permanent. All washed, rinsed,
and ready to comb, I used my new self-assertion, and picked
up a comb to start briskly combing my hair all by myself, with
plans I would be the one who rolled it on bobby pins.

Combing my hair, I became baffled. I could not get the
comb to pass through my hair. Tangles I was used to, but when
I tried to undo these ones, they just stuck to my comb. They
kept sticking to my comb and matting up until there was more

hair in the wastebasket than on my head. With most of my hair in the trash can, my new flashy look disappeared, and the halo of fluffiness around my face took on a shiny glow which I instantly recognized as scalp. I was all forehead. I was put out when I started to roll my hair with ten bobby pins, only to find out that five would have been sufficient to roll up the tiny dab of hair left remaining on my head.

There was the new "me" -- practically no hair, but plenty of forehead and nose. All my life my nose had been referred to by my closest kin as an "Irish Tater" nose. Now the word Idaho could be added to "Tater" for a more apt description.

At this stage in my improvement, my scar on my forehead had settled into the shape of a fiery "W." I wondered if it had taken that shape to remind me of my adolescent days when I day-dreamed that wicked women lived exciting lives; as a youngster, I thought how wonderful it would be if I were one. Now I thought the best I could now aim for was for that "W" to stand for Winsome instead of Wicked. But, taking another glance at the new "me" in the mirror, I realized, even with my vivid imagination, it would be stretching it to describe me as looking winsome.

Instead, I found myself looking at a nineteen year old girl, crippled, with a few hairs, a lot of nose, a forehead that had a glaring ugly scar and missing two teeth, which I had finally lost as the result of my car accident. I never could keep my mouth shut. When the collision occurred, I must have had it in its usual position -- open. The smash-up must have made me close my mouth faster than I ever had. I still talk too much, but the one time I did keep my mouth closed for any length of time, it cost me a couple of teeth!

With most of my hair gone and no idea if it would ever grow back, a mouth full of broken teeth, plus a scarred forehead, I should have been morbid with my spirits hitting a new low thinking that life for me was just not worth the effort. But that thought never entered my nearly bald head. Fall had arrived with its chilly nights. I was too busy trying to keep my head warm to be worried about my sad appearance -- an appearance I had wanted to improve. Drafts, particularly at night, were my big worry. I could not bear the idea of having to wear a night-cap. Visions of my four quaint Phifer old maid great-aunts who went capped day and night crossed my mind. I knew the family would all too readily identify my looks with them the minute I donned a night cap.

I solved my drafty-head problem at nights by extending my blankets from floorboard to headboard with me lying in between like a mummy, practically suffocating but warm.

After the failure of my hair to add glamour and pulchritude to my appearance, the thought occurred to me that my hair had never been my best feature. My figure and clothes were.

The first fall after my accident, I was wearing pant suits thirty years before they came into style for women. Looking at the 1939 fall issue of Seventeen Magazine and seeing the outfits for college girls, a pang of sadness came over me when I realized that I would never again shop for college clothes, or for any type of clothes. The more I looked at the sharp styles, the uglier my lounging-type pant suits looked. I took stock of my figure and came to the conclusion I could expose more leg and not look too bad. I thought, "I'll buy a new wardrobe."

I did not go shopping, my sister did. Living in Atlanta, Beatrice sent me boxes of clothes to select from that had been given out "on approval" by Davidson-Paxton, J.P. Allen and Rich's. Later, I started window shopping in Charlotte at Ivey's, Belk's, and Efird's. When I saw a dress or a hat that I liked in the window, a clerk would bring it out to my car for me to look at or to try on. I was always lucky getting a parking place right in front of the stores. While parked and shopping, it was like a reception as a number of my out-of-town friends would be shopping and would stop by my car for a sidewalk visit.

Imagine getting to park on a main street in front of a city department store today, and pointing at a dress in a window display and saying, "Let me see that one," and a clerk running out with it hanging over her arm! I still maintain that the late '30's and early '40's were the best years to be handicapped, if you had to be handicapped.

Looking at and trying on clothing in my car never embarrassed me. One clerk helping me did lose her aplomb when I tried on an off the face hat she was showing me. Attempting to flatter me with her sales talk, she commented, "This hat sets off your pretty hair line." And then she looked as though she could go through the sidewalk when she took in my forehead scar. She looked so remorseful that I bought the hat to ease the situation, even if all it did was frame my forehead disfigurement.

I never did make it back to the college scene as a student in my stylish clothes but I was observed by Bessemer City High School students. Recently a BCHS graduate remarked to me, "While I was in high school, I never thought of your handicaps. Seeing you in your pretty clothes, I always envied you, your cars, and the places you went. I never realized the undercurrent of sadness about your condition that could have surfaced but never did."

Not all people shared that young girl's opinion of my crippled state. When others were consoling me, I often found myself trying to help people accept my plight with less disturbed emotions, especially the elderly. Older citizens and young children, I soon found out, will tell it like it is. Could be the older ones are straightforward because they are tired from their years of having to hide their true feelings, while the younger ones have not caught on to the art of subtlety.

The older a person was, the more terrible he or she thought my situation, and they always told me so in a frank manner. I kept trying to convince them that life for me was not all bad.

But oldsters are hard to change in their way of thinking, and they are set in their notion that a handicapped life is a most terrible thing.

Elderly strangers have joined well-known acquaintances in giving me sympathy without my even expecting or wanting it. Among these strangers was an elderly apple man who sold his wares from a truck bed parked along the roadside. I came into contact with him one bright fall afternoon in my first year of paraplegia, when Wissie Gray was driving me for an outing. While we were growing up, Wissie's father was the only dad in our crowd who would turn his car keys over to a teenage girl. Frank Gray's hobby was building and racing race cars. Driving was in his blood and it rubbed off on his daughter. Wissie was always my best bet for driving me to the places I wanted to go. Driving was in her blood as well, and going places was in both our systems.

As Wissie and I rode down the highway on that bright fall afternoon with the car's top down, we saw a truck parked by the roadside. Apples, spot-lighted by the sun, were stacked on its bed, so we stopped to buy some from the vendor. The Apple Man, who had come straight out of the mountains, walked over to our car, and he took a look at me. Seeing my unbandaged scar turned even redder by the warm sun, he uttered, "What inna world happened to younse's forehead?" I felt like I was replaying a stuck record when I gave my stock explanation: "It is an injury I received this spring in an automobile accident."

He mournfully shook his head to tell me, "That's awrful. Hit's terrible lookin'." He seemed so distressed over my disfigurement that I made an effort to comfort him. I patiently stated, "It looks bad now. Give it time and it will heal and hardly be noticeable." I gave him this information in an assured manner, even though I was in full agreement with his assessment.

He emphatically answered, "Oh no it won't! Hit'll always be

thar. My Bruddar's gotta scar that looks jist as bad as yourn. He got hit inna head with a brick bat an' he's gotta-nawful scar." Nodding his head wisely, he added, "And hit never got no better, neither." He pondered a bit, and then giving me a knowing look, summed up his personal knowledge of forehead scars: "Yourn warn't git no better, neither." This he said with finality.

As we drove off, he was still sadly shaking his head and sighing over my blighted looks. If he had known how hopeless my handicapped conditions really were, I expect he would have felt a deeper concern than he did over my sorry looks. Incidents like that hardened my skin and prepared me for encounters with children, old men and women and religious fanatics.

After coming into contact with children as a cripple and suffering through their frank remarks, it is no wonder I am a writer. I had to use my imagination to make up tales to tell inquisitive youngsters -- tales I strived to make sound "cute" in order to soften my explanation, often more for myself than for the young ones. Now I have to tell it like it is. My cute little remarks explaining my condition may have worked in years past, but not anymore. Yesterday's children would bluntly ask me, "What's wrong with your legs? Do you stay in that chair all of the time?" "Can't you walk?" However, today's children have come into contact with a number of wheelchair-bound invalids, mostly in their own families. They also see wheelchair victims on television. These days I must tell the truth about my afflictions. The "Now" generation knows all about crippling accidents. When I say, "I was hurt in a car wreck," they knowingly shake their heads with understanding.

It seems many are getting hurt and crippled these days from accidents of different types, as well as health reasons and the ravages of war.

Wheelchairs have stopped being the big mystery to children that they once were. There are too many of them around these days for my chair to stand out as it once did. Young ones now accept handicaps more readily than their elders. Older people still have a tendency to commiserate with me about my "terrible" condition.

Men have been as bad as women about letting me know what a dreadful shape my life appears to them. One older man not blessed with tact, a man I had never seen before and have not seen since, let me have it between the eyes. In the course of my conversation with him, the fact dawned on him that I was married. He abruptly asked, "Does your husband still live with you now that you are crippled?" Taken aback at his crude question, I hastily pointed out that "I was paralyzed at the time I married." In shock, he exclaimed, "My. You must have had a lot of money for any man to have married you!!" Always known as being a person with a ready answer, this was one time I was dumbfounded trying to come up with a reply.

Most women are kinder. Instead of insulting me about "my sorrowful lot," they marvel at my accomplishments, especially over the fact that I am a mother. They display a great amount of interest in the fact that, as a paraplegic, I gave birth to three children. They insist these births were miracles. I have given up in trying to explain it was no miracle that I had a baby. My children were conceived, carried, and birthed just as other women do. I will concede that being the first paraplegic to conceive and give birth is something to talk about, just not to marvel over.

Then there are the religious fanatics I have to suffer with. They are the ones who see nothing but gloom and death for me in my condition. In my forty years, I wish I had counted the number of people who have asked me, "Are you ready to meet your Lord?" "Are you a Christian?" How could I answer such questions? If there is anyone who has great faith in God and His omnipotence, it is me. How could I have lived without having a faith strong enough to sustain me during the countless moments of desolate sadness I have experienced? In truth,

I may be the one who is the religious fanatic as I live with the belief that God has a master plan in which all of us have different burdens to bear.

My burden is being handicapped. When I pray, I do not think I should ask God to make me whole again. I feel I should ask Him for guidance in making the best of my situation. I am like the "lily in the field," having blind faith that God will take care of me. That is my religion and that is the way I live. That may make me look like a simple-minded person to others but nothing has ever happened to make me doubt my beliefs.

Lois's Nurse Wilmuth

8

Chapter Eight

Paraplegics are different from others, such as polio victims, arthritics and the cerebral palsied. We are a breed that has no control over our bladder or bowels. This feature of my handicap is the thing that creates my major problems. Sitting in a wheelchair and doing everything from a seated position is nothing. It is ridding my body of waste that makes an invalid out of me. Before I could continue to make any progress toward rehabilitating myself, I had to find an elimination system I could live with. When it comes to body eliminations, nobody talks about it. Everybody does it -- but nobody does it as I have done these past forty years.

Different paras handle their waste problems in different ways. I am one of the few paraplegics who underwent surgery to take care of my urine waste needs. Since I am an "oldie" and came along, as one doctor commented, before anyone knew "what in the hell to do," some doctors said "operate," and they did. Surgery was done on me. This surgery made an opening in my bladder to insert a permanent drainage tube. The opening is located between my navel and what some persons refer to as their "twat." Placed in this area of my body, the opening confuses some peekers, when they take a quick look. They think my urine is coming out of my navel.

The drainage tube inserted into my bladder handles a constant flow of urine that is collected into a rubber bag tucked inside of my underpants. This catheter inside my bladder creates different types of problems. My bladder constantly rejects my drainage tube by forming sandy sediment particles that unless

I flush them out daily by irrigating, will harden into bladder stones. I have had to use my conniving resources to solve some of my bladder problems.

These difficult situations occur at different times. When I was pregnant, I had a perplexing bladder condition, especially at the time I was carrying my first born, Sammy. I imagine I am the only expectant mother who has suffered this particular situation. Due to my stretched and protruding stomach, at times my drainage tube would pop out. This was never at a convenient place, such as while I was at home. Usually, I was in a car. When my urine plumbing system popped out while I was on the road, Sister Bea who was usually with me, and I soon made it a practice to stop at a friend's house, where Beatrice went to the door to borrow a coat hanger and a bottle of alcohol. After untwisting and dunking the straightened end of the coat hanger into the alcohol, I used it to reinsert my tube.

To think that at one time I had to be taken to a Charlotte hospital every two weeks to have a urologist perform this same procedure using sterilized hospital surgical instruments, and I did the same thing parked on a public street using an old coat hanger! Why I did not die from infection is beyond medical comprehension because my bladder carries a continuous low grade infection as it is.

Another problem involving my drainage system became more prevalent during my younger days when, with my first two children, I stayed more on the road than I did in my chair. This vexing situation was I had to find a way to empty my rubber collection bag discreetly. I always attempted to do it in a sneaky way. As a paraplegic, I learned that the best ways of handling some situations are a little like magic. We paras soon become adept at a variety of underhanded actions.

On the road, I discovered that my attempts at discreetly emptying my bag of stale urine were, I admit flops. While traveling, I did not drink my usual amount of water. This resulted in my urine having a stronger odor than it ordinarily did. To the sensitive young noses of my children, and more so to my sharp-nosed nephews, I could not pull a "wee wee" emptying sneak without their knowing it, and they weren't even peeking. Even though they could smell my action they accepted this part of me as nothing out of the ordinary. My nephews would say, "Aunt Lossie emptied her bag" just as innocently as they would say, "Aunt Lossie sneezed."

During my driving days as a young mother, filled with pre-forty vigor, I traveled with my children and my nephews along the highways from one juvenile fun spot to another. As we sped on our way, I was absorbed with keeping one of my hands on the gas throttle of my handicapped controls, the other on the steering wheel knob, and my eyes on the road. Despite my deep concentration over my driving duties, I snapped to attention at words uttered by Tommy Howard, the first grandchild in our family. Driving through odoriferous areas, Tommy, as the oldest of mine and Bea's children, felt duty bound to explain the source of every odor to anyone who would listen. "Aunt Lossie emptied her bag," he shrilled from his window seat for the whole countryside know.

Near a paper mill plant, Tommy, whose voice as a child was louder than a freight train whistle at night, yelled out to the general public, as we rolled through the foul-smelling areas, "Aunt Lossie emptied her bag!" As we drew near a chemical plant, Tommy was ready with his same free public service announcement. Driving past the beaches with their smell of dead fish prompted Tommy's announcement to go booming forth louder than the ocean waves, "Aunt Lossie emptied her bag!"

People along the Southeastern seaboard probably came to know all about Aunt Lossie and "her bag." Feeling a hapless victim of these accusations, I always made an effort to point out that in 99% of my nephew's announcements, he erred. At those points and times, I had not emptied my bag; the various environmental smells were the culprits. Associating me with bad smells, to some extent, passed away as my boisterous nephews matured through the years. Like my children, they soon learned to peg most odors to their proper sources.

I cannot complain about my method of using a small rubber urinal placed inside my panties. This adroit fashion of handling a delicate situation is convenient. And the public would never have been notified of my water plumbing system if my young nephew had not felt compelled to provide his public service announcements concerning it.

When I came home from the hospital in 1938, my urine drained through its catheter into a glass bottle that hung by my bedside. Any person who has ever visited a nursing home or a stroke floor in a hospital is familiar with seeing glass bottles decorating the sides of hospital beds.

In addition to playing a part in handling kidney waste, glass bottles are also used to observe the color, amount of urine, and the content of sediment that passes through the kidneys. Much to some patients' chagrin, these bottles are at times studied and looked over more than their torsos.

From the start of my invalid state, I started out being discreet with my drainage tube during public appearances. At my sister's wedding, and later at my welcome-home reception, and nineteenth birthday party, I had a tube and glass bottle tucked up in the skirts of my pink lace housecoat. I had to be careful as one false move and the tube would have pulled out of the bottle, which would have made for one embarrassing memory.

My first venture into the outside world, lying on an ambulance cot, and attached to a glass "wee-wee" bottle, did not exactly provide me with the bewitching glamour I strove to acquire as a college student. Now reduced to this state, I could laugh, but with more bitterness than gaiety, at remembering how at one stage of my life I had been cut down by Dorothy Parker's message, "Boys seldom make passes at girls who wear glasses." Who would ever make a pass at a teenage girl who wore a glass "tinkle" bottle?

Thanks to the craftiness of my mother and my last registered nurse, Maude Patrick, my underhanded method of voiding, (as most nice people refer to the process), was devised. Together, Mama and Maude invented a number of things for me to make my life more pleasant and to help me begin to take care of myself.

For bowel movements, I eventually worked out a system that serves me well. The process is a test in positive thinking, since with a down attitude, it could send me into resigned despair. Over a forty-year span, I have taken increasingly larger doses of strong laxatives in the early evening. I follow this up the next morning with an enema. I have used different schedules. At first, I took daily enemas, then one every other day, and now I take three enemas a week. The beauty of this schedule is that I can change it to suit my activities.

For a paraplegic to take an enema is not as easy as it sounds. Just as correct grammar and spelling are essential in news writing, with enemas, I must keep tabs on the exact amount of water that goes into my rectum because with enemas, what goes in will come back out. If I short-count the water I let flow inward and it does not all come back during my enema time, it will come gushing back out at a later, unpredictable time. And there is nothing more humiliating than a grown person sitting in "shit." Feces may be a nicer term, but "shit" is more apt for a person who has suffered through numerous humiliating experiences.

For many years, nurses performed the task of giving me enemas. But like learning to insert my own drainage tube into my bladder, I learned to insert the rectal tube into my colon by myself. I eventually took over all aspects of excreting my body wastes. This is no easy task because a paraplegic never loses their reflex actions. They stay with paras through the years, and never diminish. This aspect of being paralyzed makes taking enemas more difficult with the years. For the first twenty years of taking enemas, my bowel elimination worked like a Swiss clock. No fuss, no bother, always timed right.

From twenty to thirty years of giving myself enemas, I could sit as stoic as an atheist at a Holy Roller revival while my shit and enema water took turns belching from my rectum in perfect coordination. Soon I began to look like a Yoga convert as the time span on my bed pan extended into hours before my colon and I felt it safe to call it quits. Then it dawned on me the brand of laxative I had been taking had "played out" in my system, so I switched to another one. Now arriving in my fortieth year and having stopped any form of exercising my limbs, I can no longer sit stoical or Yogafied on my bed pan as my legs simply won't let me.

This is the point where patience is now needed since my legs act like octopus tentacles, receiving an electric shock any time I slightly touch my private parts. My legs jerk in all directions as normal reflex actions kick in. Eventually this action does calm down. While it is going on, a para has to grin and bear it.

A sense of humor also comes in good stead when a paraplegic is either sitting or lying down and some movement or pressure sends the legs jumping or moving. When these reflex responses of erratic motions start their uncoordinated dancing acts, jerking in all directions, there is nothing the para or anyone else can do but try to be amused while waiting for the legs to relax.

I have learned to reconcile myself with the different features of my condition, and now laugh them off as "just another handicap" to make light of. When situations do develop that are the result of my crippling injuries, I do not want to sit there crying over my peculiar situation. I much prefer laughing about it, and I would rather have people laughing with me than pitying me.

I am not complaining or wistfully wishing, but if I had been injured today I would be spared all of these elimination ordeals. Modern day paras do not have bladder drainage tubes, and they do not take strong laxatives and enemas for bowel emptying. When I came along with my spinal injury, there was no such thing as a rehabilitation program or therapy where paras are toilet trained. As the number grows of spinal injured persons, I feel the medical profession will continue to find ways to make living easier for us.

After forty years of trying to see the brighter side of my handicapped condition, I am glad I was trained, or rather, that I followed the procedures I do. By having my urine drain through a drainage tube into a small bag, I can always limit my water intake and I don't have to worry about emptying my bag while in a public place. I can also pick the time to take my doses of laxative for scheduling my enemas. At least I am still the boss of and not the servant of my bowels and bladder!

Thanks to my elimination set-up, I can travel and attend meetings and social functions as I desire. Traveling through the country by car, I can always pick the time and place for emptying my bowels. And on long trips, I can take several urinal bags and use them during the day to empty at my own convenience.

Numerous times I have had people ask me, "If you had a wish, what would you wish? To dance again?" My reply is, "No, my wish would not be that exciting. I just wish I could sit on a commode and have normal movements."

Buddy carrying Lois

9

Chapter Nine

Swimming had always been a sport I enjoyed. Secretly I yearned to see if I could still swim with my handicaps, but I felt no one would want to take the responsibility of taking me swimming. I silently envied my friends on their swimming excursions. Seeing news photos of President Franklin D. Roosevelt swimming also filled me with envy since he had a pool of his own. I kept thinking if a polio victim could swim, so could I, but I never had a chance to find out until the summer following my accident when Buddy Mauney, a neighbor, invited me to go swimming with him at a private pool owned by his aunt and uncle, the Carl A. Rudisills of Cherryville, a town ten miles northwest of Bessemer City.

I was thrilled at the opportunity, and doubly so since it would be a private pool in which I would get to make my first attempt to swim. I did not want to go to a public pool for my first time to swim as an invalid, so Buddy's offer was joyfully received by me because in those days only the rich had pools. As we neared Cherryville where the Rudisills had their pool at their country place, my confidence wavered. I grew apprehensive about what would happen to me when I was placed in water. When we got to the pool, Buddy carried me down its steps and sat me on an inflated rubber tube. I started paddling around in the water with my hands to renew my confidence. Finally, I got the nerve up to hang onto the side of the tube instead of sitting on it. Now with my body fully in the water, I was surprised to discover that being paralyzed made me more like a leaf in the water than the dead weight that I had feared I might be.

Instead of allowing me to sink to the bottom, water gave my body buoyancy. Forsaking the inner-tube altogether, I ventured along in the water entirely on my own. Starting with unsure movements, I soon made stronger overhand strokes, trying to do an Australian crawl. With each stroke, the rest of my body glided along behind my moving arms. My heart started singing, "1 can swim...I can swim!!!"

In my newfound joy, I turned over onto my back and changed to a back stroke. In that position, I could float but I looked like a frog swimming upside down because my lifeless legs floated in random directions. When I stopped moving my arms that had served me as propellers pulling me along in the water, my feet started drifting downwards in slow motion to the bottom of the pool. In that position, I looked as though I were treading water. Finding out that swimming and floating were still fun things I could do, I was filled with the happy anticipation of swimming the summers away.

The next time Buddy and I went swimming was with relatives of mine in Great Falls, South Carolina, on a hot summer day. Although we were there for an afternoon visit, my cousins Helen and Jean Phifer suggested we go swimming in order to cool off. Visiting there in my younger days with Aunt Essie and Uncle John Hunter Phifer, Bea and I had gone swimming with our cousins in the Catawba River that was down a slope from where my relatives lived.

On this visit, Jean suggested we go swimming in a private pool owned by one of her friends, Jean VanTyne. "The river would not be safe for Lossie," my cousin Jean pointed out. That factual statement scared me away from swimming in rivers forever. I instantly saw myself caught in a current and carried down a river stream.

As Buddy carried me toward the pool, I was not filled with apprehension as I had been on the first swimming trip. We admired the pool's tiled walls and bottom, and its pretty columned bath house at one end, when from out of nowhere a big black Newfoundland dog came rushing at us and started nibbling at my toes. I thought maybe my red nail polish had caught his eyes. It turned out that Buddy and I had not only caught the dog's eye, we had also aroused his ire. He started growling at us as Buddy kept making his wary way to the pool with me in his arms. To ward off the dog from blocking our path, Buddy used his foot to push the monstrous dog to one side. This was a mistake, a big mistake. The dog's agitation turned to anger, and he started snapping at my dangling feet instead of snarling. Buddy made a half turn in order to get the dog's teeth away from my feet. As Buddy turned, the dog made a lunge for the seat of Buddy's bathing trunks. To save his body, trunks and dignity, Buddy leaped into the pool with me in his arms. The water offered no refuge because the dog leaped into the pool after us.

Rescue came when Jean, our hostess and the dog's owner, appeared on the scene. Seeing the situation, which admittedly had elements of comedy, she shouted the dog's name, "Hans!" That word "Hans" worked like magic in turning a snarling beast into a friendly tail wagging pet begging for attention. Now that we were on a first name basis with Hans, he started trying to make up to us, asking for affection. I could not bring myself to stick out my hands with red polish on them to pat the dog on the back. I kept thinking; "Maybe it was the color of red on my toe nails that turned Hans into a snarling beast...."

That summer, Buddy and I did go swimming in public. This proved to be a fatal mistake; I did not drown there, but mortification was the thing that sank us. Since all my swimming had been done in private pools, going to a public one was a different experience. I was hesitant at mingling with the crowds there. I had mixed emotions about swimming with people I did not know and who had no knowledge of my handicaps. Buddy and I, as we always did, wore our swimsuits to the pool.

When we arrived there, Buddy thought it would be proper to talk my situation over with the pool owner. The fact that I was a cripple could make me be considered a liability risk. After hearing details of my condition, the pool's owner said, "Dive in." Looking at me, he added, "And have fun." His words put me back into a happy, carefree mood.

Walking towards the pool, we saw signs posted along the way stating, "Shower Before Entering Pool." As he carried me toward the pool, Buddy, whose spirits were also boosted by the owner's friendly consent, with good humor commented, "Let's just ignore that sign!" He did walk through some antiseptic water, as required, carrying me in his arms as he splashed through it. We were laughing over whether or not Buddy should dip my feet into the treated water when the pool owner's son appeared in our path way. He did not know my situation, but he sensed something was wrong by the way Buddy was carrying me.

"No shower" must have hit him as the thing wrong with us. He ran over to see us as Buddy was going down into the pool with me and demanded, "Did you shower?" Buddy stammered, explaining he could not go into the ladies room to shower me and I could not go into the men's room to shower with him, but Buddy was so flustered over the young man's belligerent attitude that he did not make himself clear. The son became as confused as Buddy sounded, and gave up on his questioning about shower requirements. He continued to cast watchful eyes cocked in our direction as I floated around in the pool in an inner tube. After swimming and playing in the water, the time came for us to leave, and Buddy swooped me up into his arms to carry me out of the pool to the car. As he did, the young man, seeing our movements, sprang into action again. He came running up to plant himself in Buddy's way, blocking our exit from the pool. "Can't you read the signs?" he asked with a keen sharpness to his tone. Looking around for signs, we saw several prominently displayed that stated: "No

Familiarities With The Ladies Allowed."

Blushing at reading the signs' directive, Buddy quickly started explaining my situation, saying it was not familiarity but a necessity. Before he could get the words out, the boy, with a disgusted manner, slowly shook his head. Putting one hand on his hip and the other pointing his index finger straight to the ground, he curtly said, "Put her down." With a contemptuous look at Buddy, he added, "We don't 'low that kinda stuff here."

Our confrontation with the owner's son drew an audience. As the group of bathers kept growing, Buddy made another effort to explain our actions. Before he could speak, the boy said with more determination, "I said put her down. We don't 'low no fresh carrying on." Still failing to get a word in, Buddy made his third attempt, which ended abruptly when the boy placed both hands on his hips to utter in a menacing tone, "I said put her down, now."

Defeated, Buddy started lowering me to the ground. But before I was placed there, we were saved by the son's father who came to rescue us from his son's stern management efforts. Although he explained everything to his son, along with the curious who had gathered, and apologies were made, Buddy and I still smarted with embarrassment. From that experience, I felt I knew how Adam and Eve must have felt being ordered out of the Garden of Eden. This incident shut the gates on public pools for me forever more.

Still filled with the desire to swim, I thought of the ocean. I said to myself, "Nobody owns it. I won't have to ask anyone's permission to enter its rolling waves." With this thought in mind, I decided I would try my luck there. Knowing I could handle being in fresh water, I was ready to tackle the briny sea.

Going to Myrtle Beach, South Carolina, soon became a summer excursion for me. Maude Patrick, my pretty nurse (who was also the wife of my doctor), doubled as nurse and chaperone for our beach trips. When Maude accompanied a group of us girls to the beach, she took along her young son, Charles Hughes, who had a head full of blonde curls. As the mother of an only child, Maude enjoyed the picture her son made when she had him dressed with his curls brushed in place. When things did not suit Charles on our beach trips, he would give us the ultimatum, "If you don't, I'm gonna mess up my hair!"

Now that he is over six feet tall and weighing more than two hundred pounds, I wonder if Charles ever recalls the times when the only avenue of protection he had against an array of girls was his threat to "mess up" his hair?

Leaving for the seashore, we loaded the phaeton convertible with girls and swim suits and folded the top down, then headed for Myrtle Beach. We left around midnight in order to travel at a leisurely speed and reach the beach by sunrise. Along the route, we stopped for coffee breaks at truck stops that stayed open all night with their juke boxes going full blast. These places were usually sprinkled with young boys our age who were "hanging out" at the stops. These boys were not bums, but usually college boys home for the summer with idle time on their hands. We made friends with people who seemed to be happy as we passed along in the night.

In the summers of 1940 and 1941, the Depression was behind and Pearl Harbor in the future. These were days when most people seemed to be living the good life while they could. Young Americans were enjoying their peaceful world because no one knew when our shield of isolation would crumble, and the United States would spill over into the war that was raging across the Atlantic.

These days Myrtle Beach was like a country village sitting by the seashore. A visit to the pavilion was like a homecoming event. The college set from the Carolinas gathered there, with almost everyone happy at seeing the faces of friends pop up in the crowds. Beachcombers were exciting fixtures for us girls, with their hair bleached bone-white from the sun, bodies golden brown, set off by skin-tight white swim trunks and crosses on gold chains dangling on their bare chests.

The warnings against getting too friendly with beachcombers made forming new male friends at the beach a problem, since most of the boys lounging along the ocean strip seemed to fit the stock beachcomber description.

While I was skeptical of beachcombers, I had no fear of the rolling surf when I faced it for the first time as a paraplegic. This fearless feeling made me become more adventuresome. As I was carried onto the beach, I was placed at the edge of the breakers where the waves would wash over me as they came into shore. To let me join in their fun jumping in the waves, both girl and boy friends carried me farther out, or rather helped to guide my buoyant torso deeper into the ocean where my jump-helpers placed their hands around my waist to give me a slight upward lift as waves raced by.

Our jumping activities moved us more and more toward the open sea. I felt confident that if my helpers would turn me loose, I could float back to shore on top of the waves. This confidence inspired me to float all by myself on a rubber raft in the sea. That ride resulted in the sea defeating me, turning my stays at the beach into sunbathing excursions instead of surfing occasions. I became a female beachcomber forever -- but one without blonde hair or a bare chest!

While I was on the raft, a big wave loomed in my direction, overturning me as I tried to hang onto it. I ended up under the raft and I could not find my way to the top of the surf. I became confused and was not able to figure which direction was up and which was down. Flashes of child-like thoughts passed through my mind as I floundered around. I asked myself, "If I go down, will I be in China?" I did not want to be a pioneer explorer. All I wanted to do at this point was to return to dry land on the eastern shores of the United States. I finally emerged from the salty brine, looking like a minnow that should be tossed back into its watery home.

After this incident, my confidence in the sea vanished. I became content, from then on, to sit on the sandy beach and to leave the swimming and jumping waves to others.

Sitting or lying on the beach in the sun dressed in either sun suit or swimsuit, gave me an opportunity to admire my feet. In my younger paraplegic days, I had a nurse to exercise my legs and to rub my afflicted limbs with alcohol and baby oil so my feet with their ten toes looked as pretty as my hands with their ten fingers. Sun tanned from riding in convertibles with the tops down, my matching color of toes and fingernails complemented my tan. It is strange what years will do to feet, paralyzed feet in particular.

I have found out that my feet have aged faster than my hands or face. What had once been pretty feet are now drawn inward like a TV cowboy's, and my feet have drooped more than my bosoms. My toenails, once being painted a pleasing color, still get special attention because they grow in a downward direction and have to be frequently trimmed. Recently, a five-year-old girl saw my naked feet and turned to her daddy to exclaim, "She has old feet!" I could not argue with that statement!

It was at the beach where I first learned how insidious pressure sores can be. In addition to large waves, I discovered sand could be dangerous for me, too, after sand caused my first pressure sore. While I sat letting breakers cover my body at the shore line, sand washed inside of my bathing suit, where it rubbed pressure against my bottom. Between my wet suit and the scratchy sand, Maude spotted a raw spot caused by the combination.

It was short lived because she immediately started treating it before it grew into a major sore spot. I have been lucky during my years of paraplegia as I never suffered pressure sores or ulcers until I had been paralyzed for thirty-five years. The ones I did have develop were the result of my carelessness.

Although I avoided getting into the water or sitting on the sandy shore line, the ocean has stayed a thing I never tired of looking at. Even after I was married and became a mother, I stayed as thrilled as a kid when our family headed for the beach. When my children were younger, I was fortunate to have an ideal place to stay as an invalid. My mother's cousin, Ida Neisler of Kings Mountain, had a large two-story house on the oceanfront at Crescent Beach, South Carolina, which she turned over to my family each summer for a stay at the beach. Her house was equipped with a wooden boardwalk that led down to a gazebo by the shore. I could roll in my wheelchair down to the gazebo, where I sat in comfortable shade while fanned by the ocean breeze to watch my children and others playing in the surf and sand. While at the beach, supplied with the comforts of life and surrounded by my family, I felt it was one time that life could not have treated me better.

Lois rides a buggy

10

Chapter Ten

Living in a town where the railroad tracks cut the business district down the middle, I grew up with trains and I love them. Bessemer City gets "all shook up" each time a train passes through because the city sits on rock stratum so when a train comes along, the whole town shakes and the residents shake with it.

Passenger trains always fascinated me. The sound of the lonesome whistle of a coal-burning locomotive moaning in the night was romantic to me as a young girl. Crossing the tracks in the heart of town to get from the north side to the south side, I never fretted as I stood waiting for a passenger train to pass. The crowded coaches first caught my attention, then the Pullman cars with their sleeping berths. My eyes were captivated by the dining car with its diners eating leisurely meals. Such glamour those train passengers seemed to have! And if a club car were tagged on at the end, I wondered, "What could get any higher than that for high living?"

Riding trains was a part of my youth with long trips to Louisiana, New York, and Washington, and later to Atlanta while I was a college student. When we Sexton kids were young, we traveled as one big happy group with our coach-load of passengers. The conductor always chatted with us as he made his way through our cabin, his gait set to the motion of the train.

Small for my age, I was able to pass for the age of six for an extra year, allowing me to still ride the rails for free at age seven. I felt proud when I did reach Year Six, which created a problem the time I rode free illegally at Age Seven en route to Louisiana. The conductor asked me the stock questions posed to youngsters, "How old are you?" Which put me into a dilemma because I wanted the whole world to know I was seven -- just not the conductor! I handled the situation shyly, or should I say slyly, by passing the buck to my mother. I replied to the conductor's question by turning to my mother and saying, "Mama, you tell the conductor how old I am." Unnerving situations like this have come up throughout my years. Thinking fast and in a sly manner has been a handy trait in my crippled state.

This was the only upsetting moment I experienced on a train until I rode the Southern to Atlanta alone as a paraplegic. That train ride is one I will always remember!!

After Beatrice's marriage, and while she was living in Atlanta, my friends and I kept up a steady flow of traffic between Bessemer City and Atlanta. Anytime I wanted to go to Atlanta, there was always someone ready to respond favorably to my invitation to be my driver. When my class at Agnes Scott was to graduate in the spring of 1940, my family decided I should make a visit with Bea so I could see my former college classmates before they scattered off seeking their futures. (A future to the majority of them was a husband!)

The only flaw about making this trip to Atlanta was that no one was available to drive me. However, this major problem was solved when someone suggested I take the train. That settled the decision quickly, so plans were made for me to ride the train to Atlanta, traveling alone.

The plan was that someone would carry me onto the train in Gastonia, and when I reached Atlanta Beatrice and her husband Carl would meet me at Peachtree Station. On my return, Carl would put me on the train in Atlanta and Mama would have someone pick me up when the train arrived in Gastonia. What could be more simple?

With my schedule worked out, and Beatrice and Carl notified

when to meet me, a friend carried me onto a day coach headed to Atlanta. Without any ado, I was soon traveling on my first train trip since becoming an invalid. As the train headed to Bessemer City en route to Atlanta, I eagerly peered out the window as I waited to pass through my hometown. When the train did whistle through Bessemer City, I anxiously gazed out hoping that someone I knew would look up and in surprise see me, an invalid riding on a train all by myself. None did and that was a disappointment.

As the train rocked toward Atlanta, I sat in my seat all dressed up for my trip, spring hat on my head, lunch bag in my hand, and my luggage overhead. I felt like a child who had been parceled off by itself for the first time. I ate my lunch before I reached the South Carolina line, looked at my magazines, and answered the conductor's questions. Conductors had always been friendly toward me but the one on this trip seemed more curious than friendly. Looking me over, he could not detect anything wrong with me. This puzzled him because he had seen me carried onto the train. The train was just beyond the South Carolina border when he started talking to me. Answering his barrage of questions, I wracked my mind to think of evasive answers I could give him without having to come out and say the words, "I am a cripple."

At that time I realized I was a cripple but never said the words -- I did not want to say them and I didn't!

My train ride took place during the days I would rather act and talk like an idiot than to say I was paralyzed. Because of this reluctance, I will have to admit at times I stammered. For instance, when I was sitting with other wall-flowers at a dance or party, and some boy who did not know me or my condition walked over to strike up conversation and asked me to dance. Sometimes while I was in the process of thinking up an excuse, the boy would try to pull me up with his hands. Trying to prevent myself from falling to the floor as the boy pulled, I really did look spastic.

I did not look spastic on the train to Atlanta, but I did look dumb as I sat there trying not to share my case history with the conductor. Soon I began to feel foolish, which prompted me to level with him and explain that I could not walk. The conductor, now in accord with my situation, asked, "Have you made arrangements for someone to meet you?" I assured him, "My sister and brother-in-law will meet me at Peachtree Station."

After my soul talk with the conductor, I started getting nervous with apprehension. I knew my sister's history of arriving late. She is the type who operates on the notion that if she mails her Christmas cards on Christmas Eve, they will arrive at the proper time. Knowing this, as we neared Peachtree Station my nerves started getting edgy, real edgy!

This was one time, however, my sister had made a concerted effort to start for the station early. The only trouble was she was going by Atlanta time, which in those days was an hour later than Southern Railway time. Consequently, when the train rolled into the station for a brief stop, no smiling faces were there to greet me.

Different thoughts flashed through my mind as I sat there, an unclaimed passenger. My disquieting predicament brought back the memory of one of my uncle's sisters who was crippled and chair-bound. When she had become paralyzed from a spinal tumor, her husband put her on a train so she could visit her people. The husband went to get magazines before the train started and was never seen again. Would this be my fate?

Tensely I sat there, conscious of having everyone's eyes on me -- the conductor, the passengers, the brakeman, and the engineer who had received the "hold the train" signal. All eyes joined mine as I anxiously peered down the long tracks to the steep steps leading up to the station. Filled with intense anxiety, I hurriedly cast appraising looks at my fellow passengers.

My heart fluttered in dismay when I realized the futility of my search. Not a one of my traveling companions looked capable of rushing to my assistance. As my spirits sank in despair, I heard running steps and family members gasping for breath as they came running to the waiting train to claim me.

When I gave my brother-in-law Carl Howard an extra big hug in appreciation as he picked me up off of the train seat, the train crew and passengers, now relaxed from their tension, almost broke into applause. In the distance, even the train whistle seemed to give a merry "toot-toot" as the now relieved conductor wiped his sweaty brow, and the engineer continued the train on its way to the main terminal, running behind schedule but freed from its passenger's complications.

Now that I had arrived at my destination, my sister invited my former classmates to her house for a visit with me. It was good to see them. Oddly, I did not experience the sadness I thought I would knowing they would graduate as Agnes Scott College Class of 1940 while I would always be classified in ex-'40 status. It was astonishing how much had changed in a two-year span. Nothing seemed the same in 1940 as it had in 1938. I realized my college friends and I had drifted apart, and that we had lost a great deal of our close bonds. Their interests were different from mine. In their world, they planned and looked toward the future. In my world, I lived from day to day because my future promised no tomorrows. I did not visit the college campus -- that time or ever again. I was afraid a visit would be too painful, and make me realize my college days could have been the happiest of my life.

My return trip turned out to be more relaxing and enjoyable than the one to Atlanta. A male friend traveling in the same direction took care of me. With him, I was safe from the conductor's attention. Instead of sitting in the day coach, I sat in the club car where at last I was achieving a childhood dream. I was dressed in my Sunday best, thrilled over my setup, and filled with interest in my fellow passengers. I just could not keep my eyes off the train club car set, who in my youth I had termed as "high livers." In my childhood I had stood on the outside watching them with envy as they sped through my hometown. Now I was one of them! What a joyous feeling I had!

Like dressing up to ride on trains as I thought young females should, I dressed up for other occasions, such as buggy riding and skeet shooting. Later that summer, I went for a buggy ride. That fall, one of my group's activities was skeet shooting. I enjoyed both.

The buggy ride took place one Sunday when John Stiwalt, a farmer who lived on the outskirts of Bessemer City, loaned his horse and buggy to Wissie Gray, Buddy Mauney, Jimmy Ritter, and me to use on a picnic outing. For our first time riding in a buggy, Wissie and I dressed as we thought ole timey buggy picnic bound girls should dress. Copying heroines in Western movies, we wore wide-brimmed bonnets tied under our chins and straw hats. Jimmy and Buddy did not share our enthusiasm for dressing up and did not go as far as Wissie and I did in our buggy riding roles, but they did wear straw hats.

I do not know who was braver: Mr. Stiwalt for turning his horse and buggy over to Greenhorns, or us "city kids" who had never before driven a horse-drawn vehicle. If the horse had cut up on us, I do not know what we would have done. But Mr. Stiwalt assured us his horse was gentle, which the horse proved by safely pulling us to a spot located near a creek where we spread our lunch. I had a folding canvas back prop that I used when I sat on the ground or the sandy shore of the beach, which we had packed along with our picnic lunch.

While we ate we turned the horse out to graze just like in the movies. I was a little leery the horse would run off and the others would go running after it, leaving a helpless me all my myself beside the babbling brook.

The horse was either gentle or lazy because it simply just

munched grass in the same spot where the boys had tethered it.

During the afternoon, we took turns holding the reins and posing for pictures. When my turn came to pose in the buggy, holding the horse's reins as though I could drive it, I wondered what I would have done if the horse had taken off in double time. If the horse had bolted and taken off, its strength would have lifted me right up and off my buggy seat. Fortunately, the horse cooperated in all we did -- or at least it was well trained in pulling a buggy. Jimmy kept claiming he had handled horses growing up on a tobacco farm in the Eastern part of the state, and that he knew horse language and reins action. But we thought he was just putting us at our ease.

When we took a skeet shooting trip out in the country, most of the girls joined me wearing the same type of outfit I wore. One semester while I was a college student, I took horseback riding lessons. I spent more money on my riding habit than I spent on a horse, because I was terrified every time I sat in the saddle and the riding instructor handed me the reins. For my lessons, I bought riding breeches and kneehigh boots. I later wore these for skeet shooting. Mama had bought me a .22 rifle to use for target shooting, which I took with me when I went skeet shooting. With the only body control from my shoulders up, just picking up a gun would topple me if I did not balance my body carefully. To hold the rifle up straight into the air and steady it, I had to really get myself in a balanced position. Fortunately, I was able to handle my rifle in good stead and never accidentally shot anyone -- but I never hit a clay disk either.

I fared a little better shooting empty cans in target practice, as the cans could be set up on an eye level, where I could use my elbows to help me prop and aim my rifle. However, in skeet and target shooting, as in most things, I did more talking than I did shooting. It was fun for me to dress up and go with the crowd. Doing the same things walking people did made me feel more content with my lot in life.

Lois travels to Washington, D.C.

11

Chapter Eleven

In my invalid state, I was not homebound; I traveled. One place I went to more than once was our nation's capital, Washington, DC, a place a person keeps going back to because one never sees it all. Although I had lived there one summer as a young girl, after becoming a paraplegic I made three more trips to see a little more of the capital. To most conventional people, I might be considered a fool for going there at all, let alone three times. But I grew up "young and foolish," and as I grew older, I did not outgrow my foolishness.

For my first trip to Washington, I went as a crippled 19-year-old chaperon, traveling through the country by car. For my next trek, I rode as a passenger on an over-crowded train during World War II, so Beatrice and I could observe our National Capital during war times. On my third visit, I drove my son Sammy and my nephew, Tommy Howard, on an educational trip. And I do repeat, I was a plumb fool according to some conservative thinkers, forever heading north to the political heart of the United States in my crippled state.

WASHINGTON TRIP NUMBER ONE

On the first trip to the capital as a 19-year old invalid, I was fresh into dresses from my pants suits, but I was still being arm carried. On that trip, I shared chaperon duties with my Mother. We furnished a car for the privilege of chaperoning a group of elementary school boys to the National Patrol Boy Convention. Mama and I were involved with school patrol boys since my first cousin A.G. Phifer was one. At times A.G. and his older sister Marie made their home with us after they lost both parents as children while living in Texas. Mama had a soft spot in her heart for her orphaned niece and nephew. In addition to them being orphans, their father, Grady Phifer, had been the brother who introduced my mother to my father. When Uncle Grady was working in Louisiana for a lumber company, Mama went to visit him. My father worked for the same company, which ended with my father meeting and marrying my mother. So when Grady's only son A.G. and his patrol buddies wanted to go to the convention and needed chaperons, Mama offered our car and us with it. The school found a driver in high school senior Charles (Chuck) Clemmer.

Along with driving, Chuck took on "carrying" duties for me. Our trip and tour of the capital went smoothly until we had a wreck. Just as before in Georgia, this wreck involved my car and a truck, a produce truck this time. The location of the collision was the same, an intersection, and once again the truck was at fault. As before, I was the passenger most "shook up." Fortunately, this time when the two vehicles collided at right angles, the truck did not swing broadside from the impact as the one in Georgia had done. In our Washington wreck, the truck's front bumper hit and held fast to our front bumper.

The first wreck I was in took place on a sparsely traveled road near Stone Mountain, Georgia, and passing traffic did not generate a great deal of commotion. But in almost the heart of Washington, our wreck created a traffic jam. It did not take long for the police to arrive on the scene and get traffic moving, the junked produce truck picked up out of the road, and the injured female sent on her way to the hospital.

As I was sitting in the front seat, my vulnerable forehead got it again. The impact had thrown my body forward and my head smacked into the windshield, making a spider's web of the glass with a clump of my hair caught in its center. My injury was minor with the skin around my old scar slightly cut and bleeding. I looked worse than my injury warranted. Although I apparently had no serious injuries, the policeman investigating the accident thought I should be examined in the emergency room of a nearby hospital.

Following the Law's order, Chuck carried me into the hospital's emergency room and placed me on an examining table, where a young intern, displaying a pronounced professional air, came in to examine me. I told him I did not hurt anywhere, and he took my word but did feel around, to some extent. In a matter of minutes, he told me, "No bones are broken." Then turning to a nurse who had been assisting him, he said, "Put a bandage on her forehead." That ended my examination.

After the nurse had finished carrying out her order, Chuck picked me up to carry me back to our car, which had suffered only minor bumper damage. Walking down the hallway, we met the intern who had examined me. He stopped to cast a puzzled look in my direction. Reading his facial expression at seeing me carried by a handsome high school football player, I read disapproval. His look told me he thought I was making a big ado over a slightly bruised forehead, using my automobile shake-up as an excuse to act cute. As we left the hospital, I wondered if the intern's professional aplomb would have been shattered if he had found out his girlish-acting patient was paralyzed over two-thirds of her body, and he apparently had not gotten a hint of it during his examination because the words "paralyzed," and "my former accident" were never mentioned!

Another incident concerning our Washington accident that could be termed "amusing" took place after we returned home. A local garage had repaired the slight damage to our car. Filling out the insurance claim sheet, my mother had included an item of five dollars as the costs of having my forehead attended to. When the claims adjuster came to our home, I was sitting in our yard with a group of friends. Grace Gamble, a physically normal girl my age, was lying in a hammock while I sat on a lawn chair with my legs crossed and wearing high heels. (Having my legs crossed gave me more body control and balance.) The adjuster, seeing Grace lying in the hammock, assumed she was me and walked over to her to introduce himself. Workers at the garage had warned him that I was an invalid. As he shook hands with Grace, she set him on the right track and he made his way towards me in a flustered manner. He looked at me, sort of gulped, and hurriedly held out the papers for Mama to sign, which she did. He left in a rush.

Later, I found out what had made him so nervous and hasty to leave; when he returned to the garage, he told the the workers there what a shock he had received when he looked at me and saw my scar, still red and glowing with its new skin. Knowing our claim had included five dollars for a head injury, the adjuster kept exclaiming, "Five dollars for that scar?!" The garage men laughed and told him not to feel too pleased because that scar had been there for a year.

WASHINGTON TRIP NUMBER TWO

While my brother-in-law Carl Howard was serving with the U.S. Army in the European Theatre during World War II, my sister and her infant son Tommy left Atlanta to come live "for the duration" with Mama and me in Bessemer City. At the same time Bea and Tommy moved in, I lost my good friend Caroline Mauney to the War Effort when she left town in the early days of the war to work in Washington, D.C. Caroline wrote for Bea and me to come for a visit. Sharing an apartment with a girlfriend, Caroline offered us a free room. Since Bea and I both were anxious to see the capital during its war time fever, we accepted Caroline's offer. Buddy, Caroline's brother, agreed to go with us to help carry me. In addition to seeing his sister, Buddy also wanted to see more of Washington, little dreaming that before the year ended, he would be a midshipman cadet at the nearby U.S. Naval Academy.

Washington bound, we boarded a day coach in Gastonia that had Standing Room Only. Boarding the train, Bea carried our luggage and my backless, folding camp stool I used for traveling. Buddy carried me, and I carried our train tickets. For seating, Bea sat on the luggage, I sat on my stool, and Buddy leaned on the crowd. Time flew by for us as we joined in with the singing and merriment of the travelers, who were mostly military servicemen, some with their wives and children. Although it was a jolly crowd composed of young people, we realized some of the servicemen had left their homes and families and were headed for active duty overseas. As seats became open and the train continued North, mothers traveling with their babies were given priority seating.

Several servicemen gallantly offered me their seats, but I would have felt petty if I had taken them up on their offer. Their travel was essential, mine was for pleasure. Consequently, sitting for a number of hours in a cramped position left me with puffy ankles when I arrived in Washington, but they disappeared after a good night's sleep.

During our brief stay, we tried to take in as much of the city as we could. Even though this was war time, Washington was crowded with tourists, mainly servicemen and their families. In each building we visited, I used a wheelchair that the building furnished for the aged and infirm. After going from building to building, my foot-sore fellow travelers started eying my wheelchair with covetous looks.

Moving from one building to another, I would exchange the wheelchair for my camp stool and sit by the street curb while we waited for the speeding taxis to stop. Getting one to stop became a miracle. To expedite the process, Buddy and I decided we would put on an act that would attract a taxi driver's eye and thus we might stand a chance of getting a cab. Buddy held me in his arms by the curb with my legs positioned like normal legs should look. In this pose, I used my thumb to hail a cab. A similar routine worked for Claudette Colbert in the movie, It Happened One Night, but it did not work for Lois Sexton in Washington, D.C. Taxis kept going in all directions and they were always full. With such fast moving action, no one took time to glance my way. I was obscure. This allowed me to cover the entirety of Washington without attracting any curious stares. I almost felt normal.

While we were in the hub of the nation's government, we wanted to see some of the men who planned the action. Laura Coit, a friend from Agnes Scott, invited us to lunch at the Mayflower Hotel. Laura had been working in Washington long enough to be able to point out the men who were molding our country's destiny. When the time came to place my order, I do not know what prompted me, but while dining in a place where I had the opportunity to eat "fancy food," I ordered rabbit, which I ate for my first time. And to think I lived in an area where rabbits hopped in free range day and night! Anyone who heard my Southern accent and saw what I was eating could easily tell what part of the country I came from!

Beatrice and I were happy to renew our friendship with Laura, who had been the college student body president in 1938, the year of my accident, and who had briefly dated our Uncle Robert Sexton. A brilliant girl, in college she had appeared bookish. In Washington, she looked glamorous, with her clear blue eyes framed by her naturally wavy blonde hair now worn at shoulder length. That was our last time to see her. Through mutual friends we heard that before the year ended, Laura had grown depressed and formed a habit of going to the train terminal to watch trains come and go. One day she ended her life by leaping in front of a train. She had everything to live for, and I have often pondered Laura's sad fate.

Following our lunch at the Mayflower, we traded taxi-power for horse-power that evening — real horse-power -- to ride to a popular eating place in a horse-drawn phaeton with the top down and the coachman wearing a top hat. Fancy! After dinner (this time I did not order rabbit or 'possum), we had the coachman drop us off at the Statler. Buddy carried me into the lobby where our group sat for a short time to watch the comings and goings, and to observe the people who were the reflection of the tempo of war-time Washington.

After our crammed days and nights, we were ready to return home. When we arrived at the train terminal, we were happy to find our trainmen had arranged an extra service for us. In addition to providing a wheelchair for me, they let us pass through a special gate for us to board an air-conditioned coach before it was time to open the main gates.

Once we were on our way headed south for home, we noticed an odd thing. The train was not crowded as it had been when we headed North to Washington. Later, we realized we had seen part of the population shift that took place during World War II as folks transitioned from the rural South to the Northern industrial centers. All we were aware of at the time, however, was realizing how lucky we were to have seats in an air-conditioned coach.

WASHINGTON TRIP NUMBER THREE

I took the responsibility of being a mother in a hard way, especially with Sammy, my first child. I let him command a great deal of my attention and anxieties. Mama, like a number of other grandmothers, had a mental block when it came to remembering how to take care of babies. Beatrice, as a veteran mother with one child, gave me advice. In addition to having Beatrice's guidance in child-rearing, I read books on child care. The early years of a child's life, I learned, were important in molding his future years. I felt ready to mold Sammy and Tommy. When Tommy was six and Sammy four, I read stories to them about wild animals. They were fascinated to hear about tigers, lions, elephants, and snakes. This was before television had become a household fixture. The boys had only seen these exciting creatures in books. As I read, I thought, "Why not let the boys see real wild animals, like the ones in the National Zoo in Washington, D.C.?" After all, I reasoned, I now had a car with hand controls I could drive, and I needed only a little help getting in and out of my car. Talking to myself (which I have a habit of doing), I said, "Lossie, you can be the one to drive those boys to Washington."

When I shared these thoughts to Mama, she was ready to start packing. Mama, who was always set to spring at the word "go," was all for our making the trip with the boys. Like my husband Bill, she thought I could do anything, except Bill had his doubts about my ability in one field, and that happened to be my driving. I think it is the male in him that makes him leery of his wife driving. As we started studying road maps, Bill told us he felt dubious over our handling two frisky boys, and he felt real certain that I could not drive that far without anyone to help me. Mama was not as dubious as Bill, and she let the trip get longer the more we talked about it.

Loving flowers as much as she did, she asked, "Why not go by Wilmington to see the azaleas there, and then get to Washington during the Cherry Blossom Festival?" That sounded good to me. The more we planned our trip, the less we worried about it being my first long trip with me the only driver in the car. Before we left, I felt confident that our trip would not be anything unusual for a crippled person like myself.

Before we left, I remembered that when I was first hurt, along with the other dire predictions made about my future, my doctors had told my mother that I would never be able to sit riding in a car. They suggested the front passenger seat be removed and a wheelchair bolted there, and I could be tied in it for riding. And here I was, not a rider tied in a wheelchair, but the driver. I reckon the reality of my starting to drive in 1947 made me giddy and my mother happy.

I soon took it for granted that it was nothing unusual for me, a paraplegic, to drive two young boys on a long trip along with an adult who had never learned to change gears. Mama was not mechanical.

With my folding wheelchair in the trunk, we started off full of confidence and gay spirits, on the first of what would be many long trips with me as driver. The boys were locked into the back seat of the car, and a keen switch was positioned within easy reach of my mother's right arm. We were ready to take off to see flowers and lions.

When we reached Wilmington, North Carolina, to get some of the pent-up energy worked out of the boys, we let them kick their heels and squeal to their hearts' delight in high octaves while splashing in the ocean. When the boys started turning purple from the surf's spring chill, Mama and I brought them into our motel room to dry them off. We said silent prayers that our charges would not develop sore throats from being exposed to the weather of Cruel April.

That night, I drew Tommy as my sleeping partner. An overly active child by day, he carried his energy to bed with him at night. His sleep pattern was to roll, groan and squirm. Touch him in his sleep, and Tommy would jerk up in bed with his fists flying. Later, according to information garnished at a price from a pediatrician, it turned out Tommy's night actions were brought on by "just plain ole pinworms." That night, Tommy slept in his usual sleeping pattern, and I accidentally touched him. He sat up in bed, thrashing his arms in all directions. To get him to calm down, I woke him up. In an excited voice, he told me, "Aunt Lossie, I dreamed a man was after me!" I replied, "You did?" In a puzzled tone he answered, "Yes, and he was chasing me with a pitchfork."

Teasing him, I said "Why Tommy, that sounds as if the devil were after you!" Tommy's black eyes grew brighter, as he nodded his head in agreement and exclaimed, "Yes." It was the devil and pinworms, both after Tommy.

The next morning Tommy pulled a devilish act. It occured as I sat alone in the car while Mama marched the boys with her to Orton Plantation. She had enticed them to look at the Antebellum mansion with the prospects of seeing fish in a pond of backwater. It was not long before Tommy came running back to the car, all out of breath, and excitedly told me, "Aunt Lossie! Aunt Lossie! Sammy fell into the fish pond!"

Sitting there helpless in the driver's seat, I had horrible visions of my son lying at the bottom of the black swampy backwaters, while water lilies floated overhead unperturbed. Before I went all-out in keyed-up distress, Sammy came walking up to the car, dry. Tommy gave an impish grin, delighted over the traumatic response I had made to his impulsive imagination, one that at times flared up more on the satanic side than the angelic.

After that incident, I was happy to get our car loaded and headed for the zoo, leaving Wilmington, azaleas, and backwater behind. As we rode along the roads of eastern North Carolina, we saw numerous peanut fields and started to smell peanuts. Mama and I commented that we did think it a little strange that the air should smell like peanut butter. A glance to the back seat explained the odor. The boys had taken a jar of peanut butter from our lunch box and had it smeared all over them as well as a good portion of the back seat.

Cleaning up peanut butter was minor trouble compared to what took place later. When we arrived at the ferry to cross the Chesapeake Bay, we had a tedious wait for the ferry to come in. The boys had nothing to hassle over as they both had outside window seats. Always resourceful finding something to get into a stir about, the boys discovered they had only one pencil to share between them, and they were not in a sharing mood. First they fussed over ownership of the pencil. Then they put their words into action. When Tommy discovered he had the pencil in his possession, he figured the best way to keep it away from Sammy was to put distance between them. Since there was not enough space for distance inside the car, Tommy created more space by hopping out of the car and running with the pencil between the parked cars waiting in line for the ferry's arrival.

Mama, an old hand at running down children, leaped out of the car to chase Tommy. As the chase began, the ferry landed and cars started speeding off of it. With half my passengers out of the car, my line of cars started loading onto the ferry. I was placed in a quandary. In a matter of seconds, I had to decide if I should forsake my mother and nephew and proceed onto the ferry with only a four-year-old ambulatory for assistance...or should I sit still and tie up traffic headed onto the ferry? Before I had to make this hard decision, Mama returned to the car with Tommy in tow. As we drove onto the ferry, Mama was giving her first born grandchild what he deserved, as Sammy held the pencil. But Tommy did get the pencil in the end. The young cousins, close as brothers, could not stand to see one another chastised. To even the score of Tommy's licks from Mama's switch, Sammy gave the pencil to Tommy.

It soon turned out that frisky boys were not our only problem. Another set-back, besides juvenile ones, developed when my sidekick, Mama, started having painful catches in her side. She started limping after leaving Wilmington. Her limp became more pronounced and painful the closer we got to Washington. This was a situation for us to worry about. We were hundreds of miles from home, a car filled with two tired and crippled adults, plus two spirited boys who had too much energy.

A big question arose as mama's hip aches became more painful: "Were we going to make it, as we thought when we left home full of confidence, or would we fail, as my husband predicted?" We decided to push onward toward our goal. Talking it over, Mama and I agreed we hated to disappoint the boys when we were near our destination. As we pushed on, with Mama the suffering martyr, the younger ones, sitting in the back seat, became weary of the long hours shut up inside a car. That prompted them to start calling Mama and me "Ole Grandmas," which Tommy associated with "dirty" words. This idea developed when he first called my mother "Grandma," and she reacted in alarm quickly shushing him and saying, "You must never say the word 'Grandma.' Say 'Mama Anne.'" Sammy, who looked upon his older cousin as an idol, took over Tommy's manner of expression talking "dirty."

To perk the boys out of their boredom, en route to the capital we rode through the grounds of the U.S. Naval Academy at Annapolis, Maryland. In an attempt to instill ambition and a spirit of achievement in the boys, Mama and I pointed out to them, "If you boys act right, someday you may be able to attend this school." The boys silently turned our words over in their minds and appraised this wonderful opportunity that could come their way in the future. Then Sammy, almost in tears, said, "But Mom. I don't want to go to a sailor school. I want to go to a cowboy one."

On this discouraging note, we arrived in Washington, D.C., to find it overflowing with school students and cherry blossom lovers. This made our search for a motel a frantic one. We ended our search by retracing our way back to Maryland, where we spent the night. The next morning, when we headed for the zoo, so did half the U.S.A. as well as tourists from other countries. We were lucky to find a parking place near the elephant house, which was the animal the boys wanted to see first. I stayed in the car while Mama painfully limped off with the boys to see wild animals.

As the boys bounced along with boundless energy, Mama had to limp faster to keep up with her grandsons. Before they reached the abode of the first animals on their list, the boys spotted a man selling balloons. Balloons had always fascinated the boys and seeing the large helium inflated balloons made them beg Mama to buy them some. Telling her grandsons that she had her hands full holding onto two energetic boys, without holding onto balloons, Mama refused and turned deaf ears to their pleas. For the boys, the balloons became an issue and soon they were outranking wild tigers and lions. Sammy started to pout, and in downcast spirits, came back to the car to sit in the back seat, where he remained silent as I rained a barrage of questions in his direction. I could not get him to budge back out of the car to rejoin Mama, no matter how hard I tongue-lashed him. In a matter of seconds, Tommy appeared back at the car and flopped himself in the back seat, looking as pouty as Sammy.

Soon Mama, in disgust, came limping back to the car. It was hard to say who felt more dejected: we older ones or the two younger ones. At this stage of our mission, we let the balloons blow it for the boys seeing animals in the National Zoo; they never made it to the first animal house. Mama and I became resigned to this turn of events. More tired than angry, Mama locked the car doors and I cranked up the car to head South to return home, at least according to the road sign that stated "U.S. Highway 1....South." But with all the circles in Washington, D.C., I kept looping onto the road that had an arrow pointing "North." Caught in traffic, we passed the area where the Cherry Blossom Queen reigned several times as we seemed to keep going in circles. Just as a balloon vender appeared on the scene, I hit the lane of traffic that did indeed head "South."

When we arrived home, we found the homefront as usual. Annette, my two-year-old, came toddling out to greet me with spots all over her body: the chicken pox. And when Bill heard how our visit to the National Zoo had come to an abrupt end, he felt compelled to tell me, "That is just what I expected!" with a pleased look on his face.

After that last trip with the boys, Washington, D.C. became off limits for me. I was through with it. I felt so strongly about not going back for another visit that when Senator John F. Kennedy invited North Carolina editors for a presidential campaign luncheon, I stayed home. Later I regretted this because if I had gone that time, I would have been left with a more memorable feeling for the capital than my last trip with two spoiled brats!

Lois and Buddy watch the Carolina Cup from the platform that Pinckney built

12

Chapter Twelve

As I turned from a teenager into my twenties, a number of people came along who helped me live a happier life with my handicap. One appeared when I least expected it. On a rainy night in 1940, a stranger stepped into my life and removed the daily sameness from my activities, as he carried me in his arms down wonderful paths of diversions. He came with a knock at our front door. Standing there in a slow drizzle was my family doctor and a towering young man. "I want you to meet my nephew," Dr. Patrick said. That was my introduction to Pinckney Stowe, a textile mill owner's son, who soon became one of my closest friends.

This introduction had been prompted from numerous questions posed to Dr. Patrick from his nephew. Knowing that his uncle was the doctor for a paraplegic, Pinckney had asked him details about my condition that led Dr. Patrick to say, "If you are interested in her, I will introduce you."

Pinckney's interest in me was not romantic, it was medical. A bladder stone was the thing that brought us together. The second year after I became paralyzed, I developed a bladder stone, which when removed turned out to be as large as a bantam egg. I had just had it removed by surgery at a Charlotte hospital when Pinckney appeared at my door. At that time, he was contemplating a medical career and specializing in urology -- thus his interest in such things as paraplegics and bladder stones. However, after we met, Pinckney and I never discussed such subjects as bladders or bladder stones. He merely used my bladder stone as a stepping stone to enter my life.

Being introduced to my doctor's nephew turned out to be the best rehabilitation therapy Dr. Patrick or any other doctor could have offered. Pinckney not only added fun activities to my life, he opened the door to my future career. He was a gift-giver, selecting his gifts with care and thought. The first gift he gave me was a portable typewriter, an Underwood which I still have to this day. I could not type but I set to work teaching myself.

Mama still had her typing manual she had used when she took her business course. Using it, I spent hours and hours typing drills. One sentence I typed over and over was "Now is the time for all good men to come to the aid of their country." After learning how to type, I started to write for cash and have been writing ever since.

Pinckney planned our social activities in the same manner he selected his gifts, picking the ones I could participate in with my handicap. He was in a position to be selective because Pinckney came equipped with all the extras. His special accessories included a station wagon, a Lincoln Continental convertible phaeton, eventually an airplane, plus his mother's limousine as an option for special occasions. But to a helpless crippled girl, his biggest asset was his size. Possessing a massive physique, he was a solid rock carrying me around like a rag doll.

Pinckney and I had a good time compiling the personalities of our respective friends. Our combined group of friends appreciated one another's humor, wit and, gentility. Pinckney did not generate a lot of prattle-static like a lot of others in our crowd, but he did add class to our activities.

One of my activities he added class to was my driving a car for the first time after I became a paraplegic. In addition to his mother's limousine having the first jump seats in a car I rode in, it also had the first automatic gear shift. Using his mother's car, Pinckney let me drive. As I steered the long, long car along the roads, Pinckney would apply the brakes when needed. I did not get a car with handicapped controls until 1947. By that time, controls were developed to the extent I was able to drive a car totally by myself.

During my B.A. days (Before Accident), Pinckney had known me as a flash of pastel yellow as I passed him on the highways. With him at Davidson College and me at Agnes Scott, we helped ferry students between the two colleges. As he sped by in his burgundy-colored phaeton, my yellow one caught his eye. When we passed on the highway, if Pinckney had noticed, he would have seen that an adult woman was usually among the passengers in my car when I was headed home North. To sign out for driving home, the Dean's office required us to have a female adult chaperon. Returning to college, no chaperon was needed because we were under our parent's jurisdiction until we drove back onto campus. Adult women heading toward Bessemer City were hard to come by to serve as our chaperons. To find one for our journey home, a search party was dispatched to the Atlanta bus terminal for a Christian looking woman traveling alone and headed in the direction of Charlotte. When one was found, she had a free ride to Gastonia, and at times to Charlotte.

College rules can create conniving talents in some students. This early training probably helped me survive as a cripple.

Pinckney was like people I did not know but who knew about me and my accident. Although I had roomed with his sister, Ann, at a church conference held at Davidson College while I was in high school, I had never met her older brother. Pinckney's brief interest in medicine that led him to my door also resulted in my transformation into a glamour girl. I thought because I was able to go places and do things with him I needed to fix up.

Glamour for me included such things as going to theater productions and eating at restaurants with atmosphere. The variety of eating events Pinckney took me to included a firemen's Ladies Night banquet, the first firemen's event I had attended. Pinckney was at that time a volunteer firemen in Belmont, North Carolina. Overnight, I found myself attending firemen's balls along with enjoying entertainment in Charlotte and Atlanta.

One theater production I will never forget attending is "Hellzapoppin'," that played in Atlanta. A crowd of us went to see the stage show, which was a zany production that could be compared to the "Laugh-In" television programs of the early 1970's. Seeing it turned into an adventure for me. Headquarters for my trips to Atlanta was always at the home of Bea and Carl. Going to see the Broadway show for its Atlanta performance, we arrived at Bea's in time for our evening meal. As a young housewife, Beatrice was still excelling, this time as a cook. Bea could "set a good table," but she still could not tell the correct time. She was always running late, and we ran behind schedule with her. This was the situation for getting to the theatre late to see "Hellzapoppin'."

Dressed in his formals and me in mine, Pinckney had to carry me in his arms into the theatre after the lights had been dimmed. As he cautiously made his way down the aisle with me, a man, also a latecomer, did not hide his curiosity about Pinckney and me as he walked down the same aisle. He kept getting in Pinckney's pathway and, at times, stared at us so closely that he almost blocked our progress to our seats near the stage. As Pinckney sat me down in an outside aisle seat, the man almost fell into the seat with me, he was looking at me so intently. After I was settled, the man continued down the aisle and walked onto the stage to take a seat to one side, where he read a newspaper and was oblivious of all the "hell" poppin' loose around him!

It turned out the man was an actor in the opening scene, and Pinckney and I had unknowingly helped him to start the show. People probably thought Pinckney and I were part of the act.

Along with plays and shows, sports events were high on the list of activities I enjoyed with Pinckney.

At one event in Charlotte, Jack Dempsey was a special guest. The world heavy-weight champ gave me his autograph and a newspaper reporter used the occasion to show Dempsey's compassion for the handicapped. However, in newsprint my name came out Louis Sexton instead of Lois Sexton. From this I learned just how important it is to spell a person's name correctly, even before I became a newswriter.

In the football stadium at Davidson College, there were no bleacher seats in the end zone. When Pinckney took me to games, he would park his car at the end of the bleachers where I sat in the car staying warm with the heater as I watched the game. Later, I did the same thing in Bessemer City at the high school games I covered for the Bessemer City Record, where I served as editor along with being sports, society, news, etc. writer in a one-woman operation.

Another event where I could sit in the car and still see the action was the Carolina Cup in Camden, South Carolina, where space for cars is rented for spectators. At Cups, though, I looked at the race-goers more than I did the horses jumping steeples. For one Cup Pinckney built a wooden platform equipped with hinges for folding for me to sit on. When we arrived at our parking space at the races, Pinckney took the platform and laid it across his convertible's seats and placed a folding chair on it. From my elevated position, I could watch the races and the crowd of spectators. Some of the crowd watched me.

One couple who stopped to admire my set-up was Franklin D. Roosevelt Jr. and his then wife, Ethel du Pont. I later wished after our superficial conversation that I had told him I was in the same physical shape as young Roosevelt's father. I believe if I had, the President's namesake would have held a more personal conversation with me. Even so, it was a thrill to talk to a Roosevelt. The nearest I had been to a Roosevelt before was when I was a high school student and President Roosevelt rode through Bessemer City in a convertible. One of his sons rode with him. To watch the President pass through my hometown, I sat, dangling my legs, on a retaining wall under a railroad bridge in the heart of town. When the President's retinue passed through the narrow underpass, I could have reached out and touched the President, except I was more eager to touch his son. I thought the Roosevelt boys handsome. As I swung my feet, as a teenager goggling at the Roosevelts, I never dreamed that one day I would talk to one of the good-looking Roosevelt boys.

Another sports event Pinckney took me to that I'll never forget was the Rose Bowl game at Duke University stadium in Durham, N.C., on January 1, 1942, during World War II. Right after Pearl Harbor, the Rose Bowl classic had been moved to the East coast for military safety. I thought I would never see the Rose Bowl. Along with me, Pinckney took his mother, Mrs. S. P. Stowe Sr., his uncle Mike Patrick, and my friend Caroline Mauney, using his mother's limousine. I cannot recall any details about the game, not even which team won, Duke or Oregon (Oregon State, 20; Duke, 16), but I do remember the hassle we had reaching the stadium and getting inside of it.

Being the biggest football event in the area meant that crowds of spectators had collected at the entrance gates, pushing their way inside. Servicemen tangled with civilians as they fought to get to their stadium seats. Leading to the stadium, cars were lined up like spokes in a wagon wheel, coming from all directions.

So that he wouldn't have to carry me far to the stadium, Pinckney would get out of the car at each roadblock, explain our situation to a law officer, then get back into the car and drive forward until we reached the next roadblock. This stop-explain-and-go method brought results because we eventually got to park right outside the entrance to the stadium at our ticket section.

When we arrived at the entrance gate, where Pinckney again repeated my situation, the guard, steeped in Southern gentility, offered his assistance to Pinckney by carrying the "cripple female" into the stadium. In his gesture to be gallant, the officer opened the back door of the car and started to pick up the wrong female, Pinckney's mother! Pinckney quickly explained to the officer that it was the little one on the front seat. This information did make the police guard look a mite relieved, since Pinckney's mother was the size of a woman whose son stands six feet four and carries weight proportionately to his inches and then some.

Going with Pinckney to the Rose Bowl game was my first trip to Duke Stadium. My second game there took place four years later. And as the saying goes, "It was a whole new ball game." This was after my marriage to my childhood sweetheart, Bill Smith, and after my first child was born. The reason for going to my second Duke football game was Bill was enrolled at Duke as a student. Following his discharge from the U.S. Air Force after World War II, Bill attended Duke under the GI education bill. As a student he got four tickets for us to see the Duke versus the University of North Carolina game.

Mary Alice Horsley, a childhood friend, and her date drove me to Durham to see the game. Our plan was for Bill to meet us at the stadium entrance at our ticket section, where he was to carry me to my seat. We arrived at the stadium in good spirits, which were soon dashed when Bill came hopping up to the car to meet us on crutches. He had gone to a pep rally the night before the game, and while participating in a snake dance, had twisted his "trick" knee.

He had been admitted to Duke Hospital, where he talked his doctor into letting him leave the hospital for the game. The result of Bill's snake dancing left Mary Alice's date the one to carry me in and out of the stadium, and he had been classified as a 4-F'er for military duty.

Along with having to carry me, he had to put up with other aspects of my situation.

At any game or sporting event in which I was carried in and out as a spectator, I unwittingly developed a number of friends, all inebriated. They were the ones who assumed that I, like themselves, had indulged in too much drink, and that I could not make it on my own. They were full of friendly smiles and pats on the back for me, their pats, fortunately, hitting no lower than my waist line as I was carried. This situation was always awkward. When someone was carrying me, I could not stop to explain my situation. Because of this I became reconciled to being judged falsely about my sobriety.

Getting in and out of the stadium were small troubles compared to the ones we faced on our return trip home. After the game, we dropped Bill off at Duke Hospital so he could re-enter for continued treatment; then we raced home with the football traffic, except, after darkness arrived, our racing turned to a crawl when the headlights on our car went out, along with our horn.

Without headlights and horn, our situation was frightening. Since our car troubles developed on a Saturday night we were left stranded without any garages open. Even the gas stations we passed were closed. There seemed to be no one who could come to our rescue. The worst thing about our plight was having me, a cripple, in the car. Not knowing what to do with me helped us decide we would have to make it home the best we could. So we opted for home.

Our driver tried to stay behind a vehicle traveling in our direction in order for us to share their headlights. When we started for home, our traffic lane was a solid line of cars. After our lights disappeared, so did the other cars going in our direction. We soon found ourselves driving on a deserted road, as though an official air raid blackout had been signaled. Our car made its way virtually hidden from view, silently and alone. Going through towns, we held our breath, hoping no lawman would spot us as we drove by, a black car without lights in the ebony hue of the fall night. Being without a horn was no real problem. With three voice boxes, we knew we could make a soundable racket, if the need arose, but we could not pull a Thomas Edison and make light.

Outwardly, we did try to make light of our situation, but inwardly, our stomachs were drawn into knots of anxiety and apprehension. I started to feel like everything was my fault for wanting to see a football game. I felt guilty over my efforts to try to do things normal people did. I rebuked myself for not staying in the back room like cripples were supposed to do. Then, in a spirit of rebellion I thought, "Why can't I see football games and do things like other wives can?" On that note, we handicapped travelers reached Charlotte, where we felt we were home free.

Thinking about all the things I did as a teenager, and even after becoming a married woman and a mother, I shudder. If any of my children imitated some of the crazy things I did, I would be a prime candidate for ulcers, making some fledgling surgeon rich. I cannot believe I did all the foolish things I did as a paraplegic in my teens and as a young matron. "Foolishness," would be an apt term for my early years in rehabilitation. My trouble was I stayed young in spirit too long, but the young in spirit do have more fun.

Lois and Bill

13

Chapter Thirteen

Considering that the first time I ever came face-to-face with the boy who was to become my husband we had a fight, it is surprising that our over thirty-five years of married life have been as smooth as they have been. After returning from school "up North" in 1928-29 in Castle Point, New York, where I had lived with Aunt Ede and Uncle Joe Rothman, I learned that a red-headed Yankee boy had moved to my hometown and was in my classroom at school. According to my youthful evaluation of boys, I thought Bill Smith surely had reached the cockiest phase of adolescence. I thought he acted and talked like a smart-aleck.

These traits were evident the day the 1929-30 school term opened, and the "new boy" made his fifth grade debut by skating to school. Coming to school on roller skates was an okay thing, but this Yankee kid wouldn't stop at that. He had to put on an exhibition by speed skating up and down the two steep flights of cement steps which led to our school's front entrance. Putting on such a show did impress but it did not endear Bill to the other boys. Nor did the white shirts and knickers worn by our fresh-acting new Northern classmate score points with his Southern classmates.

During the Depression, most hometown boys wore overalls or coveralls to school. His style of dress, coupled with being a redhead and a Yankee, made Bill's entry into "the group" difficult.

Bill now tells me that before I returned home, the local boys had already started giving him a hard time for being an "outsider." By the time I had settled back home in Bessemer City, Bill had taken an instant fancy to me. This attraction, I believe, was due to the fact that I had been "up North," and he hoped to become allied with me, forming a two-man team of "us" to battle "them."

That afternoon was my first chance to show Bill Smith that he was not the "Hot Shot" he thought himself to be. I was walking with two girl classmates, walking three abreast on the sidewalk with my book satchel swinging around my neck as I walked. Popular at the time were homemade, long cloth satchels that could be filled with books at either end to balance the satchel that was draped around our necks, leaving our arms and hands free of carrying books.

The first confrontation between Bill and me occurred when we three girls, Clara Withers, Martha Blakley and I, spotted the redhead skating toward us. As he drew near, I quickly yelled to my friends, "Let's lock arms so he can't get through!" With happy anticipation, I pointed out, "He'll have to go around us in the grass!" We moved fast to lock arms and form a tight line. Without breaking his speed, Bill split right through our blockade. As he went flying by me, I slung my book satchel in his direction and one end hit him across his face. In instant replay, he slapped me back, right in my face. Chagrined at the turn of events, I burst into sobs and ran home to collect instant sympathy from my mother. I told her my side of the incident. The result of my accusation made Mama speak sternly to Bill the next time she saw him.

At my urging, she also wrote a note to our teacher to ask her to please keep the new Smith boy in the classroom for a few minutes after the closing bell rang. "That way," my mother wrote, "he could not bother Lossie on her way home from school." In my hometown school, my teachers were always prejudiced in my favor with any conflict that occurred between Bill and me. As expected, the teacher complied with my mother's request. This arrangement continued for several weeks, but it did not stop Bill Smith from "bothering Lossie."

He found other times and places to bother me. During my high school years, I begrudgingly had to admit that I thought Bill was cute, good-looking, and a good dancer. Both high school and college girls liked him as a partner for the dances popular during the Big Band era, such as the Carolina Hop, Shag, Truckin', and The Carioca, a la Fred Astaire and Ginger Rogers style.

While we were in high school, I was Bill's choice as a dancing partner, and one thing that made his red-headed temperament fizzle was for me to go with another boy to a dance. Watching Bill do his fizzle was more entertainment, his male friends thought, than seeing him do the shag. This resulted in me getting early bids to dances from other boys. These previous commitments got to Bill when he later asked me to be his dance date.

I was shy in my younger years, and would have preferred to publicly admit I had an itch than to say I liked Bill Smith. My bashfulness made me an ideal target for teasing from my classmates. During our high school graduation in May of 1936, a rush of blood turned my face pinker than powdered rouge when the Giftorian passed out gifts with verses that rhymed. When she handed Bill's gift to him, it was a wedding band with a verse the Giftorian read stating, "About our Bill Smith, I hear such a funny thing, that as soon as he finishes high school, he will want this ring."

Bill still has the ring and verse. The class prophet included me in Bill's future by foretelling that in a few years, I would be a Fat Lady in a circus, and that Bill would still be my ardent admirer. The Giftorian and prophet read the future correctly for Bill and me. We did eventually get married; although I did not become a Fat Lady in a circus, I did turn into a Crippled Lady in a wheelchair, and Bill is still my ardent admirer.

To achieve the stage of marriage for me, as a paraplegic, was not an easy task. The biggest problem Bill and I had was finding people who would support us in the idea that a girl paralyzed in two-thirds of her body should marry a healthy, normal male.

A pregnant thirteen year old girl who laid the blame on an older brother could not have created a more revved-up family controversy than Bill and I did when we disclosed we were planning to marry. I did not expect our announcement to produce a rash of hugs and kisses, but I was not prepared for the explosion of objections we received. Flighty as my nature was, I could not see past the wedding band. Others could.

A volley of cold facts and hard realities about my disabilities were thrown at me. The negative list of difficulties I would face as a wife grew bigger as my family talked. My prospects of becoming a wife faded, as the fact list unfolded. My family pointed out that I would not be able to have children, keep house, cook, or take care of my husband. With these black marks facing me, I still could not see anything too bad about my "not ables." I asked them, "Who said I wanted to cook, iron shirts, clean house, have children?" In tears I told them, "All I want to do is to get married."

My tears made family members unleash the tougher aspects of being a married paraplegic. My objectors, holding back the harsher facts until now, told me, "Lossie, you will always be a financial burden, and with your limitations, you could not expect any man to love you for any length of time."

Heartbroken over these cold realities, I sobbed, "Why can I not be an exception?" I knew what they said was true, but I begged them to understand that I wanted to have my chance to live a life with meaning. I felt my family was judging Bill and me on the surface. Our relationship had stood the test of time, including my accident and a long separation during World War II.

As a fifth grade student, Bill had taken a "fancy" to me, and that fancy grew over the years. Starting in our early courtship,

Bill had placed me on a pedestal which he did not want anyone else to come near. As a teenager, I was a blithe spirit who never wanted to be tied down to one beau, one girl friend, one group. I liked everyone, and I wanted to be free to go where the whim of the moment directed me. I loved being with happy people. My yearning to bask in the warmth of a group of young folks was not diminished by my devastating accident. Although broken in body, I was not broken in spirit. I yearned to return to the mainstream of life and be with fun people. I was an eighteen year old girl, eager to live life to the fullest.

That yearning to be with The Gang after my accident made a close relationship with Bill almost impossible. He was possessive and wanted the two of us to be alone when we were together. Although this was in the late '30's, when young people were not into the "gruesome twosome" system, Bill refused to share me with a crowd, and teenagers at that time hung out in crowds.

I remained this way into early adulthood. Another factor stood in Bill's and my way; singing and dancing were Bill's favorite recreational loves. I never could sing; now I could not dance.

Bill enlisted in the U.S. Air Corps in 1940 and was immediately shipped to Panama, where we exchanged weekly letters the entire time he was at Albrook Field. He was there when our country was attacked at Pearl Harbor. When Pearl Harbor brought us into World War II, my life, like those of my friends, was completely turned around. The draft took my boy friends one by one. It was a sobering thought to know these young men, who loved life every bit as much as I did, were risking their all so that we at home could continue to live our free, happy lives.

Instead of pursuing fun projects, my interest turned to patriotic ones. In addition to selling U.S. War Bonds in booths set up in the business district, I also formed a War Bond Club in which people paid money to me weekly, until they had paid enough for a $25 War Bond. With my faulty bookkeeping and limited math ability, I was relieved to close shop when industries started War Bond Payroll Systems.

As the different civic and club groups sponsored various programs to entertain servicemen stationed in my area, I took on their projects. From time to time, I noticed the names of listed allied servicemen who wanted pen pals. Since I had never had a pen pal, I decided to develop one with a serviceman. From a published list, I selected my first pen pal, a Canadian with the Royal Canadian Air Force, who was stationed in Newfoundland. He wrote beautiful words in beautiful penmanship on beautiful stationery.

We had wonderful correspondence crossing the U.S.-Canadian border until in one letter he asked me to send him a picture of myself in a bathing suit. I decided the time had arrived for me to bring that war project to a close. If my indignation did not stop it, I felt sure that a bathing suit photo of myself would have.

From War Bonds and Canadian soldiers, I next went to work for the Red Cross, knitting drab grey and maroon colored yarn into scarves and sweaters for servicemen. Before long, I found myself wrapped up in knitting; I wanted to knit for everyone. I decided to make a sweater for Bill, which I mailed to him. Receiving my gift, Bill wrote to ask me if the article I had sent could be a pull-on overcoat. I did notice that when I knitted, the garments grew longer and longer and did not end up in standard sizes. Appraising my knitting efforts, it dawned on me that the best thing I could do for the Red Cross was to stop wasting its knitting yarn.

My patriotic zeal did not dim my happy-go-lucky outlook on life, but it did contribute toward making me become a more responsible person -- not only to myself but towards others. By the time Bill returned to the States from Panama to enter pilot training at Randolph Field, Texas, Pinckney Stowe had joined the Civil Air Patrol as a pilot. He flew out of my life forever, but not out of my heart. There is a soft spot there as I owe him a great deal for the friendship he gave me when I needed it most.

When Bill re-entered my life, he had changed. Just as I had matured, so had he. Our turbulent teenage years were behind us. On a furlough home in July of 1943, we talked about marriage, which led to the surprise announcement to our families. While Bill was in Panama, his mother had died. His father, Orion Hood Smith, lived and worked out of state. The only family members he had in the South were his sisters, Pearl and June, who lived in Bessemer City. His younger brother Robert was stationed in the Philippines.

My family members outnumbered the Smiths and outdid their objections to marriage for Bill and me. My family saw nothing but doom for an invalid female.

After Bill and I expressed our desire for matrimony, and my family members balked, I felt as though the world had forsaken me. I cried. My tears this time were the first honest heartbroken tears of my life. These tears were ones of genuine anguish, as opposed to my previous mercenary weepings. While I took to my bedroom to wail and moan, family conferences were taking place, as usual, in the bathroom with only females present. Following these discussions, Maude Patrick, who was still my registered nurse, held a conference in Charlotte with a gynecologist to discuss with him the problems I, as a paraplegic, would have in functioning as a married woman. Dr. Orion Moore had never attended a paraplegic, but he told Mrs. Patrick that he saw no reason why I could not give birth to a baby. He added his boost to romance by promising, "If she should ever become pregnant, I will handle her case."

The results of the consultation with Dr. Moore changed the picture for my family. Now everyone was all for the wedding. With everything set on "go," suddenly everyone wanted to help.

For Bill and me to tie the matrimonial knot, haste was a necessity. Bill's furlough would soon be up. When the message, "There's gonna be a wedding" hit the grape vine, it created juicy gossip that flowed county-wide.

That the crippled Sexton girl planned to get married set off a ripple of public interest. On my home front, wedding preparations took off like something hitting the fan, scattering in all directions with everyone wanting a piece of the action. Adding to the excitement was the unusualness of the event. No one could predict how the union of a paraplegic and Air Force cadet would come out. Most people thought our marriage would be like a chemist mixing two unknown qualities together, with no one to confirm whether it would turn out to be a blast or a bust. There had been cases where a married man or woman became paralyzed after marriage, but a marriage involving a permanently paralyzed bride-elect was an unheard-of event for most people.

The hurried aspect of our tying the knot added to the spirit and tempo of the occasion. Since I could not do all that was expected of an engaged young lady, a number of my girl friends offered to be my stand-ins for some of the prenuptial requirements. My ever-helpful mother felt it would be awkward for me to go to the county courthouse to get the marriage license, she offered to go with Bill to get it. This sense of helpfulness later proved a source of embarrassment for my shy and retiring mother. When she found out this duty could have been performed solely by the bridegroom-elect, she blushed. Since most of the courthouse crowd knew Mama, she would always moan with distress when reminded of the incident in later years. Eventually, Mama could laugh about the picture she and Bill made, when they stood before the Register of Deeds to get our marriage license. The mother of the bride-to-be standing beside a nervous, red-headed serviceman, who, while getting his wedding license, was so upset, he lit the end of his nose instead of the cigarette he had forgotten to take out of his pocket.

Our wedding day, July 6, 1943, fell on the hottest day of the summer. Not a soul was formally invited, but the house and yard were overflowing with perspiring guests, who had come to witness the ceremony and to wish us happiness. A love seat in the parlor had been arranged as an altar. I was placed on it prior to the ceremony. My girlfriends had helped me dress in the lace wedding gown my sister had worn when she had married five years before, to the day. So much had happened between her marriage and mine.

In that long but brief interval before the ceremony, I nervously glanced around at those standing closest to me. It seemed I saw pretty flowers and pretty girls everywhere. As I looked at my attractive girlfriends, I inwardly glowed with pleasure at the idea that I was putting the rope around Bill's neck, lassoing him in with a double ring ceremony to make it doubly tight.

To this day, Bill has never taken off his wedding band since that hot day in July of 1943 when I placed it on his finger. My wedding band is a different story. It is not because I am not sentimental, but because I am not the slip of a girl I had been. Added weight and swelling fingers are responsible for my wedding ring staying in my jewelry box more often than on my left ring finger.

Those rings eased the tension of our ceremony, and made me hide a smile when Tommy Howard, my young nephew who had to be led by his mother to bear the rings, sang with the vocalist for the ceremony. I can't imagine I was the only one whose sense of humor was tickled at hearing a two-year-old male harmonize with an almost fifty-year-old female as they sang about romance.

To exchange our vows, Bill sat on the love seat beside me. Later, he confided he was glad he was sitting because his knees were shaking so hard that he couldn't have possibly stood for our marriage. When Bill and I were pronounced "man and wife," I

looked and saw beaming faces surrounding us. I was shocked.
I remembered my sister's wedding, where sadness permeated
the service. Here I saw joyous expressions all around me. From
the way my family and friends all wore pleased looks, the idea
struck me that instead of dreading to see me get married, perhaps everyone was glad to get me off their hands.

After the reception, and I had changed into my going away
outfit, Bill and I left for a hotel in Shelby, N.C, to spend our
wedding night. When he carried me dressed in white and wearing a white orchid corsage from my wedding bouquet into the
hotel lobby, loungers could readily see we were a newly wedded
couple. No one paid a great deal of attention to the fact that I
was carried. They perhaps thought it was the bride being carried over the threshold ritual. I do not know what the lobby
group thought when Bill carried me out of the hotel the following morning.

The act of turning from a Miss into a Mistress brought about
more changes for me than just the title. During the previous
five years of being a single cripple, I had depended on the nursing care of a registered nurse. Shortly after I was married, my
family doctor died. When I lost him, I also lost my nurse, his
wife. When I no longer had Dr. and Mrs. George P. Patrick to
see after my medical needs, I had to start using self-care instead
of professional.

Without a family doctor or a registered nurse, I entered into
marriage on wheels I could roll myself. It is now hard for me
to conceive that I spent my first five years of paraplegia being
arm-carried and pushed along by others. The first wheelchairs
I was exposed to were cumbersome things with wicker fittings,
that were too big to fit inside a house and too invalid-looking
for me to accept.

I could face the fact that I was a cripple but I rebelled at the
idea of looking like one. The act of shrinking away from facing
the reality of my physical condition made me look more handi-

capped than I really was, making others push me on a chair with small wheels. I got by with living this way because it suited my style of activities; there was always someone around to carry and push me. Prior to my marriage, this kind of living sufficed because I lived each day by sitting either on my hospital bed or the seat of an automobile or in chairs at the homes of friends.

In my home set-up, I was by no means shut away from everything when I spent half my days on a hospital bed. An outside entrance door, (which most people use), opens into my bedroom from off a side patio. It took Bill a while to adjust to the flow of traffic passing through our boudoir! By pulling a curtain, our sleeping and bath quarters can be closed off from the living area. I tell people that instead of an iron curtain, I live behind a polyester one.

A corner-shaped sink that mama found at an antique junk place sits in shelving between my bed and the windows that open over our kitchen sink. This arrangement allows me to get drinking water from my sink, food through the windows, entertainment from a portable radio (now a television), and conversation by my bedside telephone. My bed becomes a workshop when a table is placed across it.

When I became a married woman, my husband was the one person who never looked at me as an invalid, but saw me as his wife who could do things most normal people do. Before our honeymoon was over, my chair with its small wheels was packed away in the basement and a standard style wheelchair took its place. This came about after Bill was pushing me, his "new bride" in my chair, and he stopped to say, "Hell, Lossie. No one has time to push you around. Get a chair you can push yourself." And I did. Starting to roll myself, I crossed over into adulthood with a totally new outlook. As I kept pushing on, I became more self-sufficient.

Although I have owned several different wheelchairs, that first one I bought is still the one I use as my "house" chair. I tell people that when it comes to wheelchairs, "I am set in my ways." I do not like changes. My "party" chair is a folding one I keep in my car to use when I am away from home.

Having taken what most folks term the Fatal Step, I earnestly went into marriage with the goal of making it a success, and to see if I could be the exception, as I had sobbed out to my family during our lengthy debate of marriage or not for me. I wanted to disprove all "not ables" that had been listed against me then. Now on each of our wedding anniversaries, Bill never fails to make the comment, "I wonder how many people at our wedding thought our marriage would last this long?"

Lois and Bea

Lois and Bill's wedding reception

14

Chapter Fourteen

Bill and I were married in name only for almost the first year of our marriage when the U.S.A.F. transferred him from Texas to Oklahoma to South Dakota. All along the transfer route, he wrote letters imploring me to join him. "I can find a cheap place to live in Sioux Falls," Bill optimistically wrote when he arrived there. Having listened to war brides talk, I knew finding a "cheap" place near a military base was a stretch. Just finding a place to live would be a formidable task.

When I told my family about Bill wanting me to move to Sioux Falls, they thought I was out of my head to think that I, a helpless invalid, could travel over 1,000 miles to be with Bill. They told me, "What would you do when you got there? You can't look after a husband, Bill would have to look after you!" As I kept bringing up the subject, the ones discouraging me pointed to my powerless state.

"You can't drive a car, your mother doesn't drive." They explained, further informing me, "No one would put you on a bus, train, or plane to travel alone more than half-way across this country." From their consensus, it looked like I would remain in Bessemer City for the duration.

As I heard all these negative points, I took a positive attitude and asked myself, "Why not??" The only receptive ears I could get to listen to my "why not" talk about going belonged to my friend Wissie (Elizabeth Ann) Gray.

She was as anxious as I was to venture Westward. Like me, she had been confined to the East coast and was ready to break out of confinement. She was not only willing but ready to drive me to South Dakota, which meant broaching the need for gas and tire stamps to Mama. She served on the Bessemer City War Rationing Board that ruled on getting extra stamps for such things as sugar, meats, gasoline, tires and heating oil.

Mama was not as willing as Wissie to go to bat for my application for the extra gas for our big trip. She put a temporary stop to our plans when she told me, "I do not have the nerve to make such a foolish request to the other board members. They would think I am as out of my mind as you are." Mama's refusal was final. But it did not deter Wissie and me in our plans. Since Mama would not ask for us, we decided we would state our wishes together to the chairman of the Ration Board and let him be the one to place our request.

To do this, we rode back and forth in front of his house late one afternoon. Our courage sank with the afternoon sun when no one opened the door to his house. As we drove by for the fourth or fifth time, the chairman of the Ration Board finally walked into the yard with his dog. We hailed him and he came over to our car to speak to us. As Wissie and I doubled up to explain our request, he listened. When he said, "I'll see what I can do for you girls," we felt like we were almost on our way West. At the next board meeting, the chairman presented our petition. The board reacted differently from what my mother had predicted and voted to give us extra gas, but not tires. They told us that if the need for tires came up, we could have the nearest Ration Board contact them.

The board did make one request. It asked Wissie to demonstrate that she could change a tire, which she did in good form. Joyous in our victory at getting gas stamps and in Wissie's flawless performance changing a tire, we did not know at that time that my car did not have a good spare tire, nor did we realize that traveling West, we could ride for miles and miles without passing another vehicle, town, or service station. The rationing of gas during WWII made the roads virtually deserted of travelers. We shared the highways with military convoys.

Now that gas stamps were a sure thing, Wissie and I started packing the Buick Phaeton from back seat to canvas top. Not knowing what to take, we took everything.

Our packing included such items as a small washboard for whoever washed, a cookbook for whoever cooked, and an army cot for whoever might have need of it. The box of grits was for Wissie and me to share, and the medical supplies were all for me. My wheelchair was the last thing packed. A non-collapsible type, we took it apart and prayed the assembly bolts would stay tied to their proper parts.

We set our departure date for a Monday in the spring of 1944. Our "Going West" day arrived and with it came rain. Wearing our spring hats with our spring outfits, the car sagging low with weight, but our spirits flying high, and our eyes weeping both sad and happy tears, we took off in the direction of Asheville, the "City In The Sky." We found it to be truly the "City In The Clouds" -- clouds of fog. We drove through fog and drizzle the entire day.

Reaching Cumberland Gap, we started looking for a tourist cabin. The one we eventually stopped at looked like a shack but the main thing we noticed was that the cabin was on ground level and we could see through the fog and rain the sign "vacancies." After seeing nothing but "No Vacancy" signs, this one looked good to us.

For me to get in and out of our sleeping abodes, I had to depend on the strong arms of male strangers who happened to be lounging around the places we stopped. Fortunately, the right kind of male was always at the right place at the right time for us. During our travels as two lone women during war times, only one male helper tried to get "fresh" with Wissie. He probably wrote me off as a dud! And only one lodging place turned us away because of my crippled condition.

Wissie and I had planned an "early to bed, early to rise"

schedule. Our schedule was disturbed our first night on the road because of the cabin's paper-thin walls. We could hear conversations in the adjoining rooms and from what we heard, we had free entertainment of an unusual theme. The place we stopped turned out to be one of ill-repute -- a whore house. It was near a defense plant, but the discussions we could plainly hear were not about military equipment.

The next morning, we left our mountain sleeping place with tired and lowered eyes. We did not want to see the expressions on others' faces as we made our departure, two women alone, the little one having to be carried! The only person to wave us off on our second day of traveling was my obliging male carrier.

Our first day we drove in rain. Our second day was through an ice storm. Finding ice glazing the pastoral countryside of Kentucky made us realize the South's early spring had been a premature gesture on the part of a fickle Mother Nature. As we slid toward the Northwest, we started encountering billowy snowflakes referred to on the car radio as "snow flurries."

To us Southerners, the snow flurries looked like a blizzard. We blew into South Dakota with the snowflakes while hearing reports on the radio of grain being air dropped from planes to stranded cattle.

Bill met us in Sioux Falls at a pre-arranged location to take us to our "cheap" living quarters, which turned out to be one of the nicest hotels in Sioux Falls and by no means cheap. Seeing our packed car, Bill said, "Pick out one suitcase each and we'll do the unpacking later." Without bothering to assemble my wheelchair, Bill picked me up and carried me into the hotel. As we entered the hotel, both Wissie and I had to hold onto our spring hats to keep the Dakota gales from blowing them to the Black Hills.

The hotel proved to be our home until we could find other accommodations. Wissie and I were not the least bit happy at being cooped up in a hotel after leaving the Sunny South. The drab, gray days that followed did not help us make a happy adjustment on our first far-away trip from home. Sioux Falls was overflowing with people, but Wissie and I, high above in our hotel rooms, did not see them. We read about them in the newspapers. From the classified ads, we discovered that people were offering cash rewards to anyone finding a place to live for the advertiser. Reading this gave us a jolt, and a bad one, as we were among those seeking a place to live. Wissie and I agreed that we did not look forward to spending many days shut up in our hotel room, away from it all. We decided to do something about it.

The day we made our decision was a Sunday. Bill was at his air base. Wissie and I looked at one another and then out of our no-view windows. I reached for the telephone directory and tackled the furnished apartment listings. This turned into a friendly business affair. Everyone I talked to wanted to prolong our conversation so that he could hear my southern accent a little longer.

As my accent kept being appreciated, it became thicker and thicker. Before long, I came to one man who answered my request for a furnished apartment in the affirmative. I could hardly believe my ears when the apartment manager said, "Yes," adding, "the people in it are in the process of moving out. You can move into it anytime now." But like the others I had talked with, he asked, "Where in the South are you from?" When I answered, "Bessemer City, North Carolina," this, as in my past conversations, failed to strike a chord of familiarity. Some of the Northerners I talked to that day had been to Florida. The closest anyone had come to Bessemer City turned out to be our apartment manager, who had been to White Sulphur Springs, Virginia. He felt right homey with us Southerners after that visit. I hated to point out to him that between Bessemer City and White Sulphur Springs are piles of mountains.

We three settled into the first apartment I had ever lived in, one called an efficiency. Even if we had paid a cash reward, we could not have found a place that better suited my handicaps. It was on ground level, and the first apartment on the right side of the entrance. Best of all for me, the living room windows opened onto a sidewalk in a residential area. I was fixed. The building was easy to carry me in and out of, and I had a window I could look out of and see people. These things meant a lot to me.

The efficiency of our apartment met the requirements for utilizing space, but it required maximum energy to utilize some of its efficiency features -- such as pulling down the disappearing wall bed, which took the strength of Bill. One day Wissie attempted to place it back into its wall repose, and I almost lost my companion.

She started to disappear with the bed. I grabbed her by one leg, and soon I was being pulled upward and out of my chair! Thankfully, Wissie fell onto my lap and the bed fell onto hers. At nights our living room turned into a bedroom, when the wall bed was pulled down for Bill and me.

The dining alcove in the kitchenette turned into Wissie's boudoir at night. The army cot became Wissie's property. It would have served her well, but, in packing, we had left out one of its main supporting poles, which we replaced with a poor substitute. Like the bed, the cot had to do a disappearing act each morning in order to give us ample living space, as well as maneuvering space for my wheelchair. The cot soon earned the reputation of being a pincher.

Wissie got pinched by it each time she put it up and took it down. I always knew what time Wissie came in from her dates at night because I could hear her exclamations as she set up the cot.

Wissie and I were ready to play house, but neither of us knew how. Now, the farthest away we had ever been from our mothers, we did not know which way to turn. Growing up, our groceries had always been done in small town style with our mothers calling their lists in by telephone, and the grocery man delivering them. Perishables, he placed inside our refrigerator and our bill he handed to us at the end of each month. Back home, we were called "charge customers."

Now living in a city featuring only cash and carry, we needed help. Mercifully, help soon came. Being friendly Southerners, we made friends with our Northern neighbors. Our housekeeping ignorance brought out their altruism. They eagerly did our grocery shopping, ran our errands and kept us company.

We soon formed a chummy circle of friends among the apartment residents.

Having lived in a large house remodeled to fit my wheelchair, I felt the closeness of our limited living quarters, especially in the kitchen that turned out to be my domain. The kitchen excelled in efficiency of space by doing away with practically all of it! There was never any problem of too many fingers getting in the pot in my kitchen. With my wheelchair squeezed into the cooking area, no one else could fit as much as a finger's worth to aid my cooking efforts.

I quickly learned about all of the problems involved in wheelchair cooking. The biggest hindrance to us "shorty" wheelchair cooks is that we have to do all our cooking, stirring, and frying on a level over our heads. In my sitting position, I am not tall enough to see what is going on inside of the cooking pots. In those first attempts, I was not sure about what I was doing, and I for sure could not see what I was doing. Consequently, I have learned to do a lot of lap cooking. To do this, I tie my legs together with an inch-wide elastic band that I call my "G" string and keep hidden under my skirts. That way I can do away with the wide gap between my knees, and by having them tied together, I can place a wooden board on them to use as a work space. When I get ready to stir a pot, I set it on my work board, so that I can stir and see what is going on inside the pot. I also use my lap board as a carrying tray, transferring different items from place to place.

This is not always as "neat" as it sounds because a paraplegic's legs will jump at the slightest jar, and as my legs have jerked a number of glasses and dishes have been broken by my system (not to mention the messes created on the floor). Nothing is worse than dropping a raw egg on the floor unless it is dropping it on the spokes and axle of my wheelchair!

I think being able to wear a "G" string above our knees gives us females one up on our male counterparts. Since they don't have skirts to hide "G" strings and various unsightlies under, I often wonder how male paraplegics manage to carry a glass of water. Without tying my legs together, I could not cook or roll around the house to do house work. This was especially useful when I carried my babies on my lap.

Without having my legs tied, the children would have slipped between my paralyzed knees to disappear on the floor. With my knees securely tied together in my efficiency kitchen, I soon became more proficient in the art of throwing, tossing and catching than I did cooking.

A National League pitcher could match my ability for discarding trash into a waste container from anywhere in the room. Or catching glasses and plates as I raked them off their high shelves, grabbing them as they fell. I admit I have had failures, such as a pound of ground coffee that fell on my head as I pushed it my way from its elevated position, scattering grounds in my hair and down inside a stove heating unit. That accident did make me and the kitchen smell good for several days. So did vanilla flavoring when it spilled on my dresses.

My cooking did not develop as quickly and as well as my aim. As a novice chef, I went strictly by the cookbook. According to the cookbook Wissie and I carried out West, the less amount of water used cooking vegetables and meats, the more nutrients, it stated, are retained. I was all for retaining as many vitamins as I could.

In my efforts as a healthy cook, my boiled peas turned out to be popped peas and my boiled corn, fried corn-flavored with charcoal seasoning. I soon learned that to cook food that others will eat, the cook has to sacrifice a few nutrients in the process.

Seeking information on Southern cooking prompted my first telephone call home from Sioux Falls. In that first call to Mama as a young bride, I called to ask her how to make buttermilk biscuits. The telephone for apartment users was a wall telephone located in the hall. It was so high that I could not reach it from my seated position. Seeing that I wanted to use the phone and could not reach it, the wife of the apartment manager said, "I'll get someone strong to hold you up to the phone." In no time she was back with help. She was accompanied by a beautician whose shop was located in the building. This beautician was a black male. He picked me up and sort of held me on his lap as I stretched as high as I could to reach the phone.

Mama, always interested in each little detail involving her baby, asked, "How did you get to the telephone? Is Bill helping you?" I figured telling her I was sitting on the lap of a male beautician would be too much. Back home a male beautician would be a rarity, and a black one, unheard of. I passed that question up.

Making the call, I felt slightly amiss over making it reverse charge to my mother, as she had taught me that long distance calls should be restricted to giving out death notices and other messages of the utmost importance. And here I had called long distance to talk about biscuits. I was getting plumb out of hand being away from my mother's apron strings!

From my first cooking experiences, I learned about more than cooking. I learned if a person wants to stay thin, they need to stay out of the kitchen.

As I started to cook, I started to eat. Not because the food was especially good, but because I hated to throw away food I had spent time and patience cooking. Leftovers turned into my enemies. I just could not throw away leftovers, so I ate them.

Along with cooking, I also learned about Northern weather. In the Northwest, it seemed as though the seasons had been reduced to two, winter and summer. Wissie and I arrived when the area was having what we call winter weather. Before we knew it, hot summer weather had arrived and without any spring softener. Overnight, snow flurries had turned into dust flurries. We did not have a chance to find out if there was such a thing as fall in South Dakota. Arriving with the hot days were Bill's orders to report to the East Coast for overseas duty.

Although all three of us would eventually be headed East, Bill had to travel with his outfit by transport train to New Jersey. From there, he had a furlough in Bessemer City prior to going back to New Jersey to wait out being shipped to parts unknown.

That left Wissie and me to make our trek back East alone, traveling again as two young women in a car and one of them a cripple. Being the crippled wife of a military man did offer some compensations. When we left Sioux Falls, we had a set of new tires and extra gas stamps to get us to North Carolina.

Since Wissie and I figured we would never be back West, we decided we should take the long way home. We wanted to see more of the Midwest. We had read in newspapers and heard on the radio about areas in the West suffering from floods and tornadoes. We planned our route home through those disaster areas so we could tell the folks back home what they looked like. Apparently, I was born with the innate curiosity of a news reporter.

We should have been content reading about such areas and left the seeing alone. In the flooded area, some roads were closed, and we had to make detours. Wind storms, we decided, were not the best force of nature to tangle with. We reached that conclusion on our first night headed home when a "blow" roared in. The windows, doors, and anything else that could rattle and shake did, and I shook with them, expecting to be blown away in the middle of the night.

Wissie had a negative reaction to my suggestion that we sleep under the bed instead of on top of it. I had read of incidents where entire houses had been swept away, leaving only the flooring intact. I felt the floor would be safer than our bed.

That was one time it was comforting to hear the wheels of large transfer trucks clicking as they passed in the night on the busy highway in front of our tourist cabin. I thought, "If those trucks are still rolling, the storm cannot be too bad!!"

When Wissie and I arrived home from our sightseeing disaster, the first thing anyone said to me was how much weight I had gained. It turned out my extra weight was not all caused by eating Western beef and corn. I was pregnant.

Bill carring Lois on their wedding day

15

Chapter Fifteen

The news of Bill's and my engagement had spread county-wide through the grapevine. The rumor of being pregnant spun statewide through gossips, spinning faster than the eye of a tornado. People just could not believe a paraplegic could have a baby. But I had all the symptoms.

Speculations were varied and wild as to what I would produce. The numbers game was against me giving birth to a normal child. Eventually, people became reconciled that only the birth itself would disclose what my embryonic product would be.

People were so busy making predictions about my outcome that they could not see my problems. My problem was that I was a twenty-six year old pregnant paraplegic who, as far as anyone knew, was the first para suffering such a predicament. I was living in a town that did not have a doctor and I was plagued with World War II shortages.

Grasping onto the promise made two years before by Dr. Orion Moore of Charlotte concerning my possible pregnancy, I went to see him at his office. Dr. Moore, who confirmed my condition, kept and delivered his promise in due time. To get to his office for routine check-ups, I had to travel over thirty miles. Not being able to drive, I had to find a driver. Not being able to walk, I had to find someone to carry me in and out of his office.

Due to war time regulations, I had to make an application to the War Rationing Board for extra gas stamps. Getting gas stamps was the easiest of my problems because of my physical situation and "delicate" condition. I qualified for gasoline beyond the allotted amount. I found a driver in my cousin, A.G. Phifer, who by now was old enough to have a driver's license. He had also grown tall and strong. In addition to driving me to Charlotte to the doctor's offices, he carried me in and out for my examinations. This arrangement was fine except the war and military draft kept draining me of my man power. Before long, A.G. received his Greeting From The President, which prompted him to enlist in the U.S. Navy.

While A.G. was joining the Navy, my sister Beatrice, her son Tommy, and a pack of bird dogs had come from Atlanta to live with Mama and me while Beatrice's husband Carl was sent overseas by the U.S. Army. With Bea as my driver and with extra gas stamps, my doctor days turned into care-free excursions. Our trips were like operating a free taxi service at a girls' school. Everyone wanted to be a passenger and all our travelers were females. Taking full advantage of the extra gas privilege, our car load of females started out early in the morning to make the Charlotte run. We made stops along the way to visit mutual friends, to shop, or do whatever came to mind as we progressed toward Charlotte and my doctor's offices.

When we eventually arrived at our destination, the first female who spilled out of the car had the task of accosting the first male who came walking along the street to solicit his help in carrying me into the doctor's office for my appointment. With the war raging and the draft in force, I was left with mostly 4-F'ers and old men to choose from.

The men did look confused when first propositioned, but after they were filled in on the details of my situation, they seemed to feel proud they could do their bit for motherhood and the Man in Service. Consequently, a lot of men whose names I'll never know, helped me have my first baby.

Meanwhile, that Man in Service, my partner of parenthood, was stationed in India with the U.S. Air Force. To have some part in the birthing process, Bill vowed to let his beard grow until the announcement of the birth reached him. It turned out that Bill had more accurately predicted what I was going to produce than folks at home. As my time extended, Bill's beard grew redder and bushier, as he sweated out the days, weeks, and months. In the diary I kept during January of 1945, I believe Bill did more "sweating" during my pregnancy than I did. Reading my diary, I cannot conceive that I was the gadabout expectant cripple. I was always eating and always on the go.

In the eighth month of my confinement, Beatrice was still helping me go to luncheons, bridge parties, and dinners given mostly for war brides. With both our husbands serving overseas, Bea and I socialized with other military wives who shared our husbandless situations, as well as with girl friends who were engaged to servicemen. In addition to these activities, Bea and I would spend the night with out-of-town friends. I now wonder about how I had the nerve to spend the night with a friend in my advanced pregnancy.

Reading about these incidents made me recall others that were just as foolish.

One of such foolish actions was making a mountain trip when I was carrying my first child. To get the extra stamps that were given for each car, we had bought an old Model-A Ford convertible, which allotted us extra gas. Painted a bright yellow, we named the Ford "Chuggy." Although riding in Chuggy was a tiring chug-chug motion, it was my favorite car. One sunny winter Sunday before A.G. left for "boot camp," our family made a two-car trip to the mountains. I rode in Chuggy with A.G. Our caravan traveled on a mountain road under construction and still unpaved, not yet touched by commercialism. We seemed to be the gravel road's only travelers. In the midst of nowhere, Chuggy chugged out and had to be abandoned until it was towed in for repairs the following day. A.G., who stayed with the Ford, put me in Bea's car for the return home.

The ride out of the mountains proved as eventful as the ride there. Bea had bought a new Packard and was not familiar with its new features, such as its overdrive gear, that meant she could coast on hills to save gas. Since the mountains were full of hills, the car was freewheeling to conserve gasoline. As we raced along the mountain slopes with Bea pumping the brakes to check speed, the car's brakes started smoking. When Bea finally got the car to stop, she pulled out the car's manual to read it for her first time. With an anxious load of passengers hanging around her neck, Bea followed Step Number One, Step Number Two, etc., and learned how to get her car out of its new-fangled gear so that we could continue home.

My mountain trips and care-free excursions to the doctor's office ended on February 8, 1945, when Dr. Moore placed me in Charlotte Presbyterian Hospital for the last weeks of my confinement. Not knowing how my pregnancy would proceed, he felt it best for me to be close by as my time drew near. The day before leaving for the hospital, friends came to see me off. Some of my callers thought I was leaving for a dangerous mission. One visitor, "Ma" White, an elderly woman, sent me into a quandary owing to my ignorance on giving birth. As she leaned toward me to get closer eye contact, I could hardly hear her, as she anxiously whispered, "Has your milk started leaking yet?" Since the birthing process was a mysterious thing to me, I started wondering if my bosoms were scheduled to give an early performance by gushing forth streams of milk!

While I kept giving guarded glances downward to note any signs of leakage, my nephew Tommy, whom I adored, added a dash of humor to my going-away tension. In preparing a layette, Mama and I had made a fancy bassinet for the blessed coming. It was in the den, so Mama took a group of well-wishers to show off our artistic talents. When she opened the den door, there was Tommy perched inside the bassinet sound asleep. He was clutching his stuffed rabbit and had a story book placed nearby, his shoes neatly placed underneath the bassinet.

As the first grandchild in our family, Tommy had my appreciation for his every action. He provided me much needed humorous diversions during the early days of my paraplegia. With his mischievous black eyes, Tommy was a born entertainer, and stayed ready to provide it for free to anyone who would observe it. His joy at entertaining was displayed one day while I was sitting propped up on my hospital bed watching him in action. He paused long enough in his act to benevolently request, "Aunt Lossie, hold my rabbit up so he can see me, too." When it was time for me to leave for the hospital, I felt a pang of sadness over leaving behind Tommy and the Good Life I had been living — petted and loved by all. I had basked in my wonderful position.

Placed in Bea's car and headed for the obstetric floor at the hospital, I found our trip to Charlotte was turning out to be the same as our usual go-to-the-doctor runs. We started out with me, the patient; Bea, the driver; Ruth Kincaid, the nurse; and Aunt Alda, the free rider. Our first stop was in Gastonia, where Bea turned over to Mrs. John Durham the money we had raised for a March of Dimes benefit. Our next stop was Lowell, where we dropped off Aunt Alda at Aunt Blanche Jenkins' house and picked up Margaret Reid as a replacement. Before arriving in Charlotte, we made one last stop in Belmont to see Sarah Beatty Sloan, one of the passengers in my 1938 accident. Our stops made a good day's work of spreading the news that "Lois Smith was hospital-bound to wait out the conclusion of her confinement." News sources in Gastonia, Lowell and Belmont helped dispatch this message.

When we reached the hospital, I was admitted and settled into my room to wait for "my time," which failed to come at first. Two weeks passed in a pleasant manner for me. Adding to the pleasant atmosphere of my stay were the nurses. Because I required special care, I had two: Ruth Kincaid was with me on one shift, and my first cousin, Mary Emma Phifer, the other shift. Ruth, a close friend, had graduated with me from high school. Mary Emma was also my age. With my nurses, I maintained a constant chatter about news from home, happenings at the hospital and details about the boys they dated. I felt once more like a college girl, with my nurses like my dorm roommates.

Another feature that helped me to feel content about my lengthy hospitalization was that the hospital staff let my visitors operate on an open door policy, so that they could visit me according to their schedules. Visitors popping in at odd hours broke the monotony.

Even with my pleasant set-up, I could still not sleep that first night. I had been told about such things as water breaking, contractions, and "the show." Not knowing exactly how these terms would occur, I was afraid to go to sleep for fear some of these things would occur and in my paralyzed condition I would not be aware of them. Lying awake, I heard the sounds from the hall floating into my room through the door which I had asked to be left slightly ajar. In the midst of the subdued hospital sounds, I heard the voice of Dr. Moore as he talked with the hall supervisor. From what I could hear of their conversation, Dr. Moore was getting a report on his patients. The nurse told him, "Mrs. Sweeney's blood pressure reads 167; Mrs. Stilwell has a fever of 103; and the one that came in late this afternoon is not doing anything."

The late arrival "not doing anything" was me! I wanted to yell to them, "I am doing something, I'm worrying!"

On my second day, I relaxed by reading two novels I had brought with me, Forever Sleep and Leave her to Heaven. When I tired of reading, I listened to my radio. Listening to Charlotte WBT, I perked up my ears when I recognized my sister's voice along with the voice of Sarah Beatty Sloan. I didn't know what type of program they were appearing on as guests, but when I heard them say something about Mrs. Donald William Smith being a patient at Presbyterian Hospital, I covered my head with my sheet to hide my embarrassment from the empty room.

Around noon on the third day, I thought I was having contractions. Dr. Moore was called in to examine me. To play it safe, he had me wheeled to the labor room, where whatever I thought had been taking place stopped. All I accomplished in the labor room was eating two hearty meals of steak and pork chops, plus having to pay for the cost of the extra nurse called in to watch me. That false reading of my body's actions made me more conservative in my future analyses.

After that first flurry of excitement from being admitted to the labor room, I settled down into a routine and made the most out of my wait. During two weeks of my sitting on Hospital Hold, friends came to see me and brought candy, salted nuts, and flowers. With my insatiable appetite, I ate everything brought to me. On the night of February 20th, Beatrice, as she had done before, brought food and guests for a room party. We laughed and talked as we ate hamburgers, deviled crabs, sandwiches, lemon pie, and pumpkin pie topped with ice cream, while drinking hard-to-get cokes. Later I paid for those deviled crabs by vomiting and having loose bowels. That turned out to be a prelude of things to come.

The following morning when I woke at 6:20 a.m. I noticed a puddle of water under me. I did not want to jump to saying "this is it" again, and told myself, "Lois, that could be urine, instead of your water breaking." All I knew about the liquid was that it had wet my bed and nightgown. When Ruth, who was still with me on the first shift, came on duty, she started the usual procedure of giving me an enema. After I was dressed in one of my gift gowns, I started making George Washington favors for a community tea to be given as a financial project by the Women's Club.

While hospitalized, I had previously made Valentine favors for another project. As I cut out red hatchets and cherries, I prayed my favor-making would not extend into St. Patrick's Day shamrocks. Sitting up in my hospital bed and making favors, I kept having a feeling of suspense that something was going to happen. At 11 a.m., I did feel a queer, different type of sensation in my stomach, one that I never felt before. Since I had been fooled before by looking in the direction of my private parts for what is termed "the show," I waited until 11:25 to take my first peek. And when I did, I saw a bloody discharge.

When Ruth came back into the room, I showed her what I had seen. She in turn showed it to the floor supervisor, and when Dr. Moore was contacted, he said, "Take her to the labor room." Shortly after entering the labor room, I experienced my first hard contraction, and with it, I had a terrible pounding pain in my head. It felt as though someone had hit me on the nape of the neck with a hammer.

To ease my head pain, Ruth was told to give me two Nembutals, which I promptly vomited up. I was given two more, but my head continued pounding and hurting with each contraction. Lying there not knowing what to expect, I fancied the idea that since I could not feel pain in my birthing organs, I was having something like an echo reaction in my head.

At 1 p.m., Dr. Moore came to examine me and reported that I was fully dilated, and he could see a head with hair on it. But there was no progress on the baby's coming out. The baby staying in one position created a waiting period, which was almost like a wake, since we had no idea knowing the outcome would be. I stayed thirsty and was given some coke, which I also threw up. Then I was given crushed ice, which I sucked on during my labor. Not being able to hold anything in my stomach made me remember how I had eaten steak and pork chops on my first visit to the labor room.

As we waited for my birthing movements to speed up, my

head kept pounding with each contraction. I later was told this was due to a high reading of my blood pressure. Along with my contractions and head poundings, I had chills and sweats -- more, I thought, from the unknown factors than from my physical condition.

After Ruth went off duty, another nurse was called in. Mary Emma had to leave for another case she was committed to. My new nurse called Dr. Moore at 8 p.m. to report, "Still no action." Dr. Moore gave the order, "Take her to the delivery room." In the delivery room, after Dr. Moore had scrubbed and examined me, he said, "Your baby is in the same position as it was at 1 p.m." After telling me that, he asked me, "Can you do without taking ether?" Then he told me, "It would be much better for the baby and you, if you did not have it." He explained how natural birth would be best for me and the baby. Since I felt no pain, I did not need anything.

As Dr. Moore worked, he explained what he was doing behind the sheet shield that left only the top of his white capped head in my view. He told me, "I will use low forceps and will make one cut to keep you from tearing." At 8:36 p.m. on February 21, 1945, the first baby conceived and birthed by a paraplegic let out its first yell. As Dr. Moore held the new born baby high in the air for all to see, the delivery room staff, all dressed in white, formed a chorus line, as they sang out, "It's a girl!" In a flash, they took another look and changed their refrain to "It's a boy!"

On his world premiere, my first-born's vocals were great, but his timing was off. He urinated right onto Dr. Moore's white jacket. Dr. Moore was so relieved that the delivering ordeal was over, he ignored the insult. He was too happy. We were a happy bunch in the delivery room, rejoicing that everything had come out right.

After Sammy was oiled and swaddled, he and I were placed on an elevator to return to my room floor. When the elevator doors slid open an audience was waiting to see my baby and me. Family members and friends had gathered there to anxiously wait out the birth. Seeing them, I grinned. Samuel Martin Smith yelled. The spectators returned my smiles while looking at me, the new mother, and my squalling newborn son. Everyone was happy to see that my baby had the proper number of toes and fingers, and in their proper places.

The nurse showed Sammy off, and he proved to be a crowd pleaser.

As soon as my mother looked at her new grandson, she rushed to the telephone to wire the news of his arrival to Bill in India. Bill still has the cablegram that turned him into a relieved and proud father -- and a clean-shaven one, since he had lost his excuse for not shaving. Mama also called Wissie Gray, who had stuck with me through the years. Wissie laughingly told my Mama, "Since Bill is in India, I'll pass out cigars for him." Then she added, "I played a major role in that birth. I'll just have to get drunk to celebrate it. I'm happy it is over with!"

My ordeal was not over, my nurse advised me. "Not until after the baby starts nursing." Fortunately, Sammy was ready to nurse and I had plenty of milk. I soon found out what "Ma" White had meant when she asked, "Is your milk leaking?" At times it did!

Although I felt fine lying in my hospital bed, my hemoglobin count was low. Dr. Moore prescribed iron and a whole blood transfusion. During the blood transfusion, I felt the same pounding in the back of my head that I had experienced in labor. That was to be my last blood transfusion.

My blood donor was a Bessemer City man, Frank Baxter, someone my family was not closely associated with. When he heard I would need blood for a transfusion, he offered his without charge. The gesture on his part was typical of the way people helped one another during World War II. At that time, practically all able-bodied male friends and family members were in service. Women were not called on as blood donors. All these factors made Mr. Baxter's offer of his blood deeply appreciated.

Having a low blood count made me cry easily. One crying spree I indulged in was the result of remarks made by my sister, a person who would never intentionally say an unkind word. But she said the wrong words for a new mother to hear. Telling someone about Sammy, I overheard Bea comment, "He is not a pretty baby." That set me off into a two-hour crying jag. Different people tried to comfort me. All I could sob out was, "Beatrice does not think my baby is pretty." I was crushed. I had been telling everyone how beautiful Sammy was. Later, when I had the opportunity to observe other newborn babies using an impartial eye, I really did not see many babies that could be termed "pretty." This made me later admit, "Maybe Bea was right!"

When Sammy was eight days old, the ambulance from Bessemer City came to take us home. Riding with my new baby, I recalled the day I had traveled in that same ambulance, returning from Atlanta as a crippled eighteen-year old girl. I thought about all that had happened to that handicapped teenager in the seven years in between those two ambulance trips.

I was amazed. My first handicapped years had been filled with a little bit of everything -- sadness, love, good times, marriage, now motherhood. Now, as a wife and a mother, I wondered what the future years would hold. For the first time, I had a real responsibility. Sammy was just an infant now, one I could hug and hold. What would it be like, when he grows older? Could I handle the role of being a mother to a walking child?

Lois and Sammy

16

Chapter Sixteen

As a spinster, I thought the man was the King of His Castle. But when I was wheeled out of the delivery room onto the obstetric floor, I soon discovered a couple's first born becomes the real Kingpin and Boss of the Boneyard. That was the position Sammy held from his first yell. Growing up at a time when senior citizens were still on the home front, his cries brought help from grandparents, great-grandparents, and great-aunts, as well as from parents, aunts, and friends. They were all willing to lend a helping hand.

With a number of substitute mothers helping to take care of him, Sammy must have cuddled upon more female bosoms than a playboy in his prime. He had so many different females tending to him that when he started going to Sunday school and his teacher asked him about his mother, he felt compelled to ask, "Do you mean my real mother?"

With all my assistants, I was never tied down to the diaper pail. I had sitters pulling full-time duty. My fostering Sammy out to all the eager hands of volunteers was an on-going joy. Although help was there, I was determined that I would do everything I was physically capable of doing in my motherly duties. I flinched at the thought of others saying, "Now Miss Anne has two babies to care for."

I was still Mama's Number One baby. Before Sammy was born, I had done freelance writing for any publication that would publish me. I was also a correspondent for *The Gastonia Gazette*, a position I gave up as an expectant mother. I wanted to prove I could function as a full-time wife and mother. I soon found life was different with a baby. Sammy, as a newborn infant, upstaged me with my friends.

Instead of coming to see me, they came to see him. I became a member of the supporting cast as our household revolved around Sammy and his schedule instead of mine.

Sprinkled among the first visitors who came to see him when we arrived home were some who still termed him a "miracle baby." There were also some Doubting Thomases who, without any show of compunction, asked me, "Did you really give birth to that baby?"

Being a mother with limited mobility, I found out that when it comes to rearing a child, there is more than one way to skin a cat, and a paraplegic has to know all of them. It took more than will power for me to accomplish motherhood. I had to plot, invent, and connive just to compete with normal people. I had to learn to be a little pushy in order to push my way through life as a chair-bound mother, and, eventually, as a career woman.

Being a mother with restricted ability did have some fun things going for it. Sammy being a breast-fed baby was a big help. It did away with washing and sterilizing baby bottles, and the task of having to warm bottles in the middle of the night. With Bill getting his discharge the year Sammy was born, I had a husband who was anxious to help out as a father. Together, Bill and I teamed up to make a good parenting twosome. When home, Bill changed soiled diapers and I always did the feeding. Bill was also the baby rocker, singing to Sammy as he snuggled in his arms.

Thanks to his handicapped mother, Sammy grew up on wheels. His first wheels belonged to my wheelchair. Instead of being walked as an infant, I drove him around. I propped him in my lap and pushed him around in my wheelchair until he could stand on his own. Carriage wheels played a big part in his early life. For the first few months Sammy slept in his carriage instead of a baby bed. During the day, he was parked in the quiet part of our house. At night, his carriage was placed by my bedside where I could pull him into bed with me for feeding and changing. Using my elbows and determination, I could work him out of his carriage nest and into my bed. After nursing, burping, and changing him, it was mercifully easier for me to slide him back into his carriage bed than it was to pull him out of it.

The carriage not only served as sleeping quarters for Sammy, it also served as his washing place. With the side of the carriage supporting my weight, I could lean down into the carriage to reach him. I oiled him as much as I washed him. I imagine we created an odd scene when I moved him from place to place. As I wheeled my chair with one hand, I pushed the carriage with the other, changing hands from time to time to keep us moving on a straight course. As Sammy grew into the stroller stage, I could pull him onto my lap and slide him back into it, much like I did with the carriage.

Wheels served Sammy well as a toddler. Using my big wheel, Sammy learned to pull himself to a standing position. I was none too pleased when he wanted to use my chair's hand rim as a teething ring.

When he began to stand up on his own feet, Sammy would stand on the foot rest of my chair so he could ride around the house with me while I did household chores. My footrest became a popular riding spot for his friends to share.

By the time I was pregnant for the second time in 1947, I felt like a veteran mother. Back then, Bessemer City still did not have a doctor. For this birth, I saw a Gastonia doctor whose office was seven miles from Bessemer City. Also, I had my husband back home to be the one to drive and carry me for my doctor appointments.

Realizing that Bessemer City was the best place for us to live, Bill dropped out of Duke University when the chance came for him to operate a variety store downtown. With Bill as my carrier, my going-to-the-doctor visits were not fun excursions like the ones I had when I was carrying Sammy. Bill made the round trips without any stops or bother, and when we reached Dr. Jones' offices, my appointments were brief and routine. Dr. Orion Moore had died, and when Dr. Jones took me as a maternity case, I think he was a little baffled over what to do with me.

My second delivery was a totally different experience than my first one. This time when I had my first contractions in the early hours of the morning, I knew what was happening. I awakened Bill, who, in a highly nervous state, drove me to Gastonia City Hospital. It happened that my cousin Marie Phifer, who had just received her registered nurse's degree from Emory Hospital, had arrived for a visit. She accompanied Bill and me to the hospital. After Bill placed me in my room, Marie stayed with me while Bill went to get my bag, which had been slung together in haste, and to fill out my admittance papers.

Right after Bill had left my room, an indifferent-acting hall nurse came into the room with a bedpan. She placed it under me with the intentions of giving me an enema to get my contractions into high gear. But after she left the room, Marie walked over to my bed and said, "You are not sitting on that pan right. Let me shift you to a more comfortable position."

When she did, she looked down and gasped, and she exclaimed, "I see hair....and it is on a head!" She went flying to find help. Nurses soon had me rolling in the direction of the delivery room, where they quickly placed me on the delivery table. Dr. Jones came rushing in while this was going on and was able to give the birth a professional finish.

He happened to be making his morning rounds when Marie started yelling "Hair.... Hair!" With Sammy, I had visited the labor room twice. With Annette, I bypassed the labor room and barely made it to the delivery room!

The return trip to my room was made at a much slower pace. As I rolled along the corridor with my stomach now as flat as a pre-teen's bosoms, several sloppy and dispirited looking women with protruding stomachs gave me envious looks while they walked up and down the hall trying to get their labor contractions to speed up.

As my newborn infant and I returned to my room, Bill was nervously pacing the floor. When he had walked up to the business desk after getting my bag, the secretary said, "Congratulations, Mr. Smith, on the birth of your daughter." Bill thought she was kidding. When he found out her statement was no joke, he almost fainted from how quick it had been. He had been told to be prepared for a long wait. He could not adjust to this turn of events.

Already in a shocked state, Bill looked even more shocked when the nurse pulled the blanket from Annette's face so that he could get his first look at our new born baby. He sort of blinked his eyes and then reached over to give me a sympathetic pat on my cheek. He made an effort to put some joviality in his voice to as he said, "Give her time, Lossie. She'll shape up and look better."

This time when I heard my new-born baby was not a "pretty" baby, I did not take off on a crying spree. I laughed instead, because by that time I knew what newborn babies looked like. And I was in a stronger physical condition than I had been after Sammy was born. With Annette, I did not even have a headache. If the doctor had permitted me, I could have left the delivery room for home.

July 8, 1947, the day Annette was born, coincided with Bill's appointment with a Charlotte doctor to correct his hemorrhoid discomfort. After we looked at Annette together, Bill left to keep his appointment, Still amazed over the birth of his first daughter, Bill told the doctor in detail about Annette's delivery. Intrigued by Bill's account, the Charlotte doctor did not charge Bill for his treatment. "That will be my gift to you as a new father," he said.

While Sammy's birth was unique with him being the first baby delivered to a paraplegic, I feel sure Annette's arrival was the first birth to result in free hemorrhoid surgery as a baby gift for the father!

As with Sammy, Annette had a family of baby-sitters and helpers. They were willing to take on Annette-duty along with caring for Sammy and me. I cannot say my set-up of family helpers was always a laughing, happy situation. At times I was threatened with mutiny, but I knew I had no place to escape and neither did they. We were all "prisoners" in our compact, interdependent family destiny. Just as I did with Sammy, I strove to be a full-time mother to Annette.

Although I discovered with Sammy and Annette that I could be self-sufficient as a mother and housekeeper, I was ready to quit proving the point. I rolled away from the majority of housework to take a turn that not only placed me in the middle of the main stream of life but also made me an integral part of it.

I had just started to do freelance writing again when a bomb-shell of luck exploded my way. I was asked to be the editor of a weekly newspaper in my hometown. A female confined to a wheelchair, attempting to make a success out of a weekly newspaper being published with a limited budget and zero circulation? It should have been a frightening adventure, but in 1957 I was blessed with good health and unbridled enthusiasm. This enthusiasm came from years of being handicapped, when, in order to survive, I had to take a positive attitude toward my afflictions; I had to think "I can" instead of "I can't."

Along with Freida Lankford, the advertising manager, the two of us did everything except set type. We held the paper together through a series of changes in ownership and a change in name. Starting off tabloid size as the Bessemer Citian, the paper is now published as the Bessemer City Record in standard newspaper size. The publisher of the newspaper chain is now Garland Atkins, a member of the Atkins family and the former publisher of The Gastonia Gazette.

In its early years, The Record's circulation kept growing while its percentage stayed static. Revenue from ads remained limited because, until recent years, our town did not boast a single chain store. It wasn't long before The Record became a one-woman operation, with its offices moving into my bedroom.

I have a typing desk, but due to its width I prefer to use the top of my hospital bed for gathering copy. I may not be the only crippled female newspaper editor, but I bet I am the only one who uses a hospital mattress as a copy desk!

I could be considered a shut-in, but with my large number of family and friends, I have a county-wide network of stringers who keep me posted on news-worthy events. After over forty years of hunting for news items, I have become psychic when it comes to knowing which stables to call in order to get the news "straight from the horse's mouth." As a disadvantaged person, I take advantage of the American spirit that makes people root for the underdog. I don't resent being an underdog -- in my career, I feel like a "top dog" doing work I thoroughly enjoy. I enjoy my news work so much I would do it for free. With it, I keep in constant contact with the world. In addition to getting all the news I can print, I learn some I can't -- behind-the-scenes details that are too "juicy" for public consumption. However, these tidbits add spice, making the conversations I have more interesting.

As an invalid with limited activities, my work also absorbs hours that would otherwise be lonesome ones.

Thanks to the super help I had in child rearing and house-keeping, I still had ample time for such things as bridge and social clubs after turning into a career woman. But before long I started feeling guilty, like I should have something more than that to show for my life -- a life that had been spared by God and nourished by my family, friends, and community. Putting aside social activities, I started doing community and church work. I headed up every charity drive that came along -- and a lot came along before the United Way of Giving was conceived.

This phase of my community services stopped when my husband said, "Cut it out, Lossie. People will think every time they see you coming, you're asking for a cash donation." After I stopped "shaking an empty tin cup on the street corners," I started serving as publicity chairman for local drives, which has turned into an on-going project for me.

The church had always been a part of my life, and that did not change when I became a paraplegic. As a "carry-in" member of First Presbyterian Church, I had Billy Gamble to serve as my most faithful carrier. Sunday mornings, he would carry me in and out of the church sanctuary, and I would carry a pillow. The pillow served dual purposes. As Billy carried me, I held the pillow as a shield over my bottom to keep everything that should not show from showing. It also was used to soften the wooden pews.

After Billy enlisted in the Army during WWII, I borrowed the arms of my married friend's husbands for church going. When Bill received his discharge from the Air Force, I became a roll-in member, as Bill pushed me to church in my wheelchair.

Marriage, motherhood, and age took me out of Young People's church activities and placed me with the Women of the Church. I eventually served as president of this astute body, although it lost some of its astuteness under my leadership. Our women's work did move along in various projects, but on a much more informal basis than had been customary. The same thing proved true when I aged into the Bessemer City Women's Club and was elected its president. At club meetings, the women came dressed in their Sunday best, wearing hats and gloves. Serving as president of such a dignified women's group should have been terrifying to me as a crippled young matron but this office did not faze me since deep down inside I still thought of life as one big, happy binge.

I stayed so busy I kept forgetting that I was extremely handicapped.

In Junior Women's Club, I served as project chairman when the club won the state project award. Our project entailed organizing the town's first Girl Scout troops. During this period, my sister Bea and I served as Girl Scout leaders. Since we had never been scouts, we had to learn what scouting was all about right along with the troop members. My troop soon outgrew me, my limitations, and the limited space in our house.

Since Mama and Bea were members, I joined the Daughters of the American Revolution. In the Southern Revolution Campaign, the Battle of Ramseur's Mill took place on property owned by my grandmother Emma Ramseur Phifer's ancestors. On my grandfather Phifer's side, his great-grandfather became a personal friend of George Washington while at Valley Forge. When Washington made a trip through the Carolinas as President, he was a guest of grandfather Major Martin C. Phifer at his home near Concord, North Carolina.

Before library systems came along with their branch libraries, our house was used as a bookmobile stop. Mama and I kept a limited number of books at our house for the public to check out. We also took requests and secured books from the bookmobile driver. This project started in the early days of paraplegia. Working as an unpaid librarian was my first venture into community life as a handicapped person. It served as my entry into the mainstream of community action.

Owing to my desire to play a part in community activities, I have been honored with plaques by several organizations. The Woodmen of the World presented me with a plaque for being an outstanding woman. The American Legion Auxiliary gave me the state's first life membership. Church Women also gave me a life membership. I am vain in displaying my honors -- I get a thrill having people like me! I especially enjoyed being named

North Carolina Handicapped Tar Heel of 1967.

Audacity and determination alone did not carry my load in accomplishing these community deeds. I had a lot of support and several factors working to my advantage, such as living across the street from my church and next door to the Women's Club building. Females could help me to those places in my wheelchair. And if stronger help was needed, Bill's place of business was just two blocks away.

The one community project I consider my Best Deed was the least appreciated at the time. I learned on this project that it is easy to do things in accord with others when they approve your actions, but when the idea is revolutionary, you might find yourself sitting alone. This project came about because of Sammy. When he entered the sixth grade, his classroom was on the third floor of West School, a brick building built in 1912. The age of the school did not bother me, but the lack of fire safety did. The wooden floors had been oiled time and again over the years. The only fire escapes were two metal slides from inside the auditorium located on the third floor. Since school officials did not trust the sturdiness of the slides, the doors leading to them were usually locked. The boiler room with coal was stored in the same quarters, located between the slides. Should the furnace room catch fire, I was afraid that even if the children did get the doors open to the slides, the metal would be too hot to use for escaping the fire.

Adding to my alarm, the electrical wiring was old. When wires for the stage foot lights were jostled, sparks flew from the naked wires. The two stairwells positioned at either end of the main floor would be useless if the third floor caught fire.

At night, I started thinking about West School burning and the third floor students being trapped inside of it. Putting my fears into action, I posted notices for parents and the local fire department to meet at the school building on a certain date for a fire safety inspection tour.

The fire chief shared my concerns when he and the volunteer firemen showed up but the only parents to turn up for the tour were Louise Bullard and Louise Moore. They both had children on the third floor. Fire Chief P.I. Harmon was the father of Louise Bullard. He and the firemen gave the building a bad fire safety report. Armed with the fire department's report, the two Louise's and I started the long process of attending meetings held by the Gaston County Board of Education, an appointed group which requests funds for schools from the County Board of Commissioners, an elected group.

Working with the Board of Education and the County Superintendent of Education, Hunter Huss, we believed we were going through the proper channels with our request to make West School more fireproof. But the proper channels turned deaf ears to our pleas. As time moved on without the Board's taking any action, the Three of us "L's" grew tougher and less ladylike. When we realized no interest was being shown, Fire Chief Harmon, the state Fire Marshal, was asked to inspect the building. He did, and his report stated the building was the worst fire trap school he had inspected. If it did catch fire, he saw no way the children would escape.

He condemned the building. With his report in hand, we attended the next meeting with confidence that action would be taken. But the school officials still gave our request blank looks. I do not know if anyone instructed us or whether we made it up on the spot, but at the meeting we told school board members that, since the State Fire Marshall had condemned it, should any child suffer injuries from the building's condition the board members would be personally liable for any lawsuits.

That did it! Action was immediately taken, and the school doors were closed. Fireproofing and remodeling work started at once. Our hounding of the school board had taken place over several months. By the time the board took action, school had opened for the 1957-58 school term. It meant that students had to be transferred from West School to church Sunday School rooms and other places for classroom space. This inconvenienced the teachers, students, and their parents. When this shifting of students to places not equipped for teaching occurred, I do not think we Three "L's" could count many supporters on our side.

In a short time, the building was completed, now with enclosed outside stairwells, fireproofed floors, new paint, a re-done cafeteria, plus better smelling rest rooms. The finished building looked beautiful. An open house was held to show it off to the public. By that time, the teachers, students, and parents were proud of the school's appearance and safety features. The cost for the work amounted to $35,000, which, even at that time, was a ridiculously low amount to save the lives of children.

During the trauma of ill feelings within the community and county, I always had the backing of my husband and mother. My home-front formed a solid line of defense backing my actions, even if they did border on revolutionary.

After the school house affair, and now that Sammy and Annette were older, I decided I would bow out of school and community projects. I thought, "I'm older. As a paraplegic, I surely will not live much longer. I've already lived past my life expectancy." I kept telling myself that I was tired of my routine life and courting the public's favor. I decided from then on, I was going to do and say exactly what I felt, and, if no one liked it, I did not care. Along with my revolutionary actions, I seemed to have turned radical in my thoughts. I smirked at thinking, "No more PTA meetings, no more fund drives, no more cookie baking"...and then I found out I was pregnant! This turn of events kept me a smiling community and school worker. It seemed as though with my third pregnancy, God had prevented me from becoming a turn-coat.

With a twelve year span between Annette and my third pregnancy, I prayed the baby would arrive before August 5, 1959, so

I would not be listed as a forty-year-old mother. Lisa did me in on that score by holding off her arrival until September 3, 1959. Now when my younger daughter asks me, "Mama, why did you pick Louisa Lucille for my name?" I quickly retort, "It is to pay you back for not arriving a month earlier than you did!" By the time Lisa did arrive, I was an over forty-year-old mother, young in spirit, but wearing out fast.

Lisa's birth was the most difficult of my three children. Not for me, but for my doctors. When I was carrying Lisa, Bessemer City had two doctors, Dr. Robert L. Moore and Dr. Roy L. Cochcroft, who shared offices and patients. They would share me as a maternity patient.

When my contractions started, both Dr. Moore and Dr. Cochcroft went with me to the delivery room. They arrived at the hospital at the same time as Bill and I, and we went on the elevator together to the obstetric floor of Gaston Memorial Hospital, a new hospital built beside the one in which Annette was born. I was pleased to have the doctors with me. I have never trusted elevators and experience horror at the thought of me, a cripple, stuck inside an elevator. Riding to the delivery room accompanied by my doctors made me feel secure. I happily thought, "If the elevator sticks, stops, or does anything wrong, I have my doctors with me, and they can carry on in case anything happens."

My doctors and I made it to the delivery room without any mishaps. But when the delivery got underway, my doctors discovered the umbilical cord was wrapped around the baby's neck. They took turns moving the baby to get it in the right delivery position. My contractions were not hard enough to bring the baby out. A lot of pushing was exerted on my abdomen, which I observed since I was giving natural birth for my third time. Finally, the baby was born as a normal delivery.

While all this was taking place, I experienced the same pounding in the back of my head that I felt when my first baby was born. This was caused by my blood pressure shooting to a high reading again, just as it had when Sammy was born. Although I felt no physical pain or tiredness from the delivery, and Lisa was a perfectly formed child, both Dr. Moore and Dr. Cochcroft advised Bill and me to call it quits when it came to having children. Their advice was accepted without any argument. After reaching the age of forty, and a paraplegic at that, who could rear more than one infant!

The day Lisa was born happened to be the night Bill was supposed to play cards and eat steaks with a group of his male friends at a place on the Catawba River. With Lisa and me both doing well, I told Bill to go to the river as planned. He did, and returned home with his pockets filled with winnings from a little card action that took place while the steaks were grilling. He won enough to pay my hospital bill.

Bill had it lucky with the birthing of his daughters, dollar wise. With Annette, he got free hemorrhoid treatment and with Lisa, he literally got free child delivery.

At the time Lisa was born, I was in my second year as editor of The Record and I was also doing freelance writing for The Charlotte Observer. When I returned to my room after Lisa was delivered, I called in an article to The Observer. At the end of the report, I casually added the information that I was fresh from the delivery room where I had given birth to a baby girl. The person taking down the account could not believe it! Neither could my visitors that afternoon when they found me typing news.

During my confinement and the delivery of Lisa, I did not miss putting out a single weekly issue, which I have not done since The Record's inception in 1957. Lisa may not have cooperated in being born while I was still thirty-nine, but she did cooperate in arriving on the day the paper had been "put to bed" for that week. That gave me almost a week to go through the process of birthing a baby and getting out the next week's issue.

In the first issue of The Record after Lisa's birth, the front page carried a photo of me holding Lisa when she was four days old. She was introduced as the weekly's newest stringer, assigned to the diaper set. That was no false statement, because Lisa went with me on all of my news beats. Since I was driving myself at the time Lisa was born, she started as an infant helping me gather the news. Equipped with diapers and water bottles, Lisa lay on the car seat beside me and slept through most of our early news gatherings.

Feeding her was no problem, she was breast fed like the other two. When she got a little older, she stood on my foot rest while I was in the darkroom developing photos. To this day, she still likes to work with photography.

Lisa completed our family. This worked out to be a good thing. Telling grown children that Mother and Daddy are going to have a baby would be almost as complicated as it was announcing that a paraplegic was expecting!

Sammy and Annette in Holland, Michigan

17

Chapter Seventeen

Nothing opened up more avenues of diversion for me as a paraplegic than the automobile. Wheeling around on four wheels attached to a chair is an okay everyday necessity, but when four wheels are on the chassis of a car, a whole new life opens up for me. Cars kept playing a major role in my life after I became paralyzed, first as a single girl and later as a wife and mother. After I was married, I found out traveling as a single female is a totally different situation than making a trip as a young mother with her family.

When I think back on the times when Bill and I set out to travel, I marvel at the fact that Bill ever got the nerve to start out with me, his invalid wife, and his babies, plus his mother-in-law. To keep Bill from having to carry the full load of wife, baby and car duties, my mother usually joined us on our trips to help lighten his load.

Remembering the image of the way my brood looked when we were decked out to travel as Bill Smith and family, makes me understand the remarks of our relatives. "When Lois and her family take to the road," they said, "they look like a group of gypsies setting out on a peddling trip!"

With our car packed to the limit and the overflow strapped onto the car's top, we did look the part of a roving sales caravan.

In terms of organization, Bill and Mama shared a number of things in common. They both strived to have "a place for everything and everything in its place." The topsy-turvy fashion of life on the road with young children was enough to keep them keyed up as high as the number of miles we traveled.

On any trip we took, it was most important to me that we had fun from start to the finish, kept up with the children so as not to leave any behind, and that I had my bowel movements at the right times and places. Mama and Bill's ideas of traveling were not as simple as mine. They fretted over what to pack and where to pack it, and whether or not the toilets at our lodgings looked clean.

When Annette was a year old and Sammy three, we started making vacation trips, with our first long one made to Rodessa, Louisiana, to see Grandpa Sexton. He had met neither my husband nor my children. Getting ready for our departure, Bill and Mama absorbed themselves in packing. They both agreed, "It is best to take too much than too little." Consequently, they took everything, and everything had to be packed. I never worried about leaving the comforts of home behind -- we took them with us!

Our packings were not the usual matching luggage and hat box cases. When the children were babies, our load included a baby bed that Bill took apart and then put back together again each night we stopped, and my wheelchair, which was unbolted and packed but not put together until we reached our destination.

Along with the bolted goods, we carried along an ice cooler, a hot plate, coffee pot, bed pan, toddler supplies, crawler supplies, invalid supplies, and clothes for the changing weather. Our traveling supplies were packed overhead, at our feet, under our feet, and we even sat on some. Numerous times, Bill issued the instruction, "Put everything you girls will need tonight in one bag." A good order that did not go unheeded, because who knows what one will need four hundred miles later?

Stopping at tourist courts, Bill carried me inside and set me on the bed, from where I could watch and yell, when needed, at the children. He then set to work putting up Annette's baby bed. After Bill got Annette in her bed, and Sammy stopped switching on the various light switches, he said to Mama, "Miss Anne, show me the bag you and Lossie will need for tonight." Mama kept pointing at bags until the car's trunk was half empty.

This did not deter Bill from his efforts at efficiency. He just simply would not give up. Each morning, he continued to ask us to pack everything for the coming night in one bag. Mama and I were complete failures in carrying out this directive.

In spite of Mama's and Bill's careful planning, we had to make two unscheduled stops on our first day of traveling. The first one involved capitulating to a persistent request from Sammy. We stopped to buy him a raccoon tail cap, a popular roadside commodity at that time. It did add a certain type of flair to our son's appearance, but one that I could not fully appreciate. The second unscheduled stop was a necessity: piddling along, we heard a terrific clatter overhead, where ropes held my wheelchair to the top of the car. The noise was the rope coming loose! We helplessly watched as one of the chair's large wheels rolled along the highway towards Bessemer City.

To retrieve my run-away wheel, Bill pulled off the road and got out of the car to go after it. He successfully caught it, but the ball-bearing casings and bolts had scattered as the wheel rolled along. Searching on hands and knees for the missing parts, Bill crawled along the shoulders of the road. Cars passing slowed as travelers gaped at Bill's actions. One of them stopped, more out of curiosity than any Good Samaritan promptings.

With our packings intact, both children accounted for, and my bowels on good behavior, we eventually arrived at Grandpa's house. At this point, Grandpa Sexton had lost his hearing and sight. But he soon knew which of his family members had arrived.

Bill put me in my wheelchair and I rolled to grandpa's side. He reached out his hand, touched my large wheel, and exclaimed, "Why, this is my Star!", a nickname he sometimes

called me when I was younger. Bill thrust out his big hand and
grasped Grandpa's frail one. Grandpa said, "You must be Lois'
husband." He could tell Sammy and Annette from their sizes.
Grandpa hugged Sammy and held Annette in his arms, something he had never dreamed he would do.

Making our visit long enough but short enough to be appreciated, we left to return home. Our crew made it back without
any out-of-the-ordinary incidents, and all members in good
shape, except for the coon's tail. Time had made it smell. In
spite of Sammy's protesting screams, we threw it into the yard,
where instead of our son and his friends fighting over it, the
dogs took to battle.

This first long trip inspired us to attempt others. The next big
one we made was to Northern Michigan, with a swing through
Canada and back home through the New England states. Now
equipped with a folding wheelchair, and the children older, we
were able to travel with some degree of dignity. With all our
luggage hidden from outside viewers, we looked like an average
family taking a Sunday afternoon ride.

The passing time, however, created new problems. Both children were walking in all directions at their own discretion. That
meant we three adults were constantly on alert, our eyes cast in
all directions. This would not have been bad, except Bill always
had me in his arms, leaving Mama to do the chasing.

Annette was the evasive one on this trip. While we were mingling in the crush of tourists at the Tulip Festival in Holland,
Michigan, Annette disappeared. I was distraught until we finally
found her in another section of the park, standing in front of
a miniature windmill and staring at a little girl her size, who was
almost a replica of herself. The little girl, whose big blue eyes
were looking into Annette's big brown ones, wore a Dutch girl
outfit. Annette was entranced with the petite girl dressed in her
wooden shoes, starched cap, and apron.

On her next birthday Annette celebrated with a party. Her

Aunt Pearl Smith made her a Dutch girl outfit to wear with wooden shoes she had bought while on a trip to the Netherlands. Annette was pleased with her Dutch looks.

While on our Northern adventure, Mama, the children, and I had a new experience: sleeping on a lake steamer. We embarked on Lake Michigan from Frankfort, Michigan, and landed at Kaukauna, Wisconsin. To make my first steamer trip, Bill, along with the help of my new folding wheelchair and a husky Swede, quickly carried me up the steepest flight of stairs I had seen since Peachtree Station in Atlanta.

From Wisconsin, we traveled to the Northern Michigan peninsula, where Bill had been born in Iron River. From there, we went into Canada. When we arrived at Niagara Falls, Annette gave us another scare. While Bill held me in his arms so I could look over the guardrail and watch the massive tumbling of the falls, we both saw Annette standing on top of the wall and leaning over the guard rail as she stared down into the churning waters. Terrified that she would lose her balance, Bill quickly plopped me down on a bench and gently made his way over to pluck Annette from her perilous perch.

The only boo-boo Sammy pulled on the trip was embarrassing us while we were eating breakfast in a respectable restaurant in Canada. Over the soft hum of voices and the brisk sound of forks hitting china, Sammy jumped up and started scratching his derriere. In a shrill voice he yelled for all to hear, "Mama. Remember those worms? They're after me again!" I did remember those worms! Prior to our trip, I had given Sammy treatment for pinworms. This treatment was the result of World War II shortages in bottled carbonated drinks.

Adults as well as children agreed with a remark one of the children made at the time, "I can't wait for the war to end so I can drink a whole bottle of Coca Cola all by myself." After the close of the war, everybody wanted to drink his own bottle of Coke "all by himself." Bottling companies could not keep up with the demand.

This inspired many people to venture into the bottling business. My brother-in-law Carl Howard was one of them. He opened a Red Rock bottling plant in Bessemer City. The children were beside themselves -- whole bottles of soda pop to drink all by themselves and all for free. Our double garage was used to store some of the surplus drinks, which made the drinks handy to the children. They helped themselves to the free sodas.

This situation resulted in Sammy being taken to a pediatrician in Charlotte, because, as Mama put it, "Sammy looks wormy." The pediatrician placed Sammy in Charlotte Memorial Hospital to get him away from the bottled drinks and started on a nutritious diet. On my first and only visit to see Sammy at the hospital, he saw me rolling along the hospital corridor in his direction and jumped into action, flinging his clothes into his suitcase. He thought I had come to take him home. When he found out I had come to visit and not to take him back, he cried.

Seeing him cry, I cried. His doctor, finding us both in tears, made a quick decision to send his crying patient home with his crying mother. In addition to taking Sammy, I took a prescription home with me to annihilate Sammy's worms. From Sammy's public announcement in Canada, I realized I was a failure as a worm killer.

After being confronted with the inopportune disclosure of pinworms' reappearance, we headed for home. Enroute home through New England, we swung over into Pennsylvania to stop in Lancaster. Our stop was meant to be for pleasure, but it turned out to be educational too. In Lancaster, we visited Ruth Graeff, a paraplegic. Through a brace salesman, I had started to exchange letters with Ruth. The salesman used Ruth as an example of someone who walked with crutches and braces. I never did accomplish her achievements. I do not wear braces but I have tried them.

With encouragement from the brace salesman, Mama refused to give up on braces for me. This resulted in my having several sets of braces hanging around unused in our basement. Mama and Bill went all out on braces. Bill built an adjustable set of parallel bars for me to use to try to learn to wear braces. After I locked knee and hip joints on my braces, I could pull myself up to walk stiff-legged between the bars. I wore different outfits to fit the type of braces I was attempting to learn to use. For the last set of braces, I had the foot support bars clipped onto a pair of men's shoes, and had to wear oversized shorts over the brace's padded hip bands.

I looked like an ice hockey goalie as I stalked back and forth between the bars! At times I ventured from between the bars using crutches. Anytime I circled through the house using crutches, I was scared I would fall over like a 2 x 4 plank.

One day while I was walking with crutches, Sammy saw me walking for the first time and exclaimed, "Mom's walking!!" I wish I could have been able to let Sammy keep his thrill a little longer, but I did not have enough confidence in my ability to use braces and crutches.

Many times when Bill was helping me, he would grab me by my hip bands and waltz with me around the room to waltz tunes, which delighted Sammy and Annette, who watched us and giggled.

I was eager to meet Ruth for the first time. Writing to her, I found out we had a lot of things in common. Although I was older than her, Ruth had also suffered her spinal injury at the age of eighteen. Like me, she had been swimming, and was returning home, and was the only one seriously injured among the passengers.

Through her, I became acquainted with Martin Clark, who was also a paraplegic. He received his spinal injury while on active duty in World War II. He was hit by mortar shell fragments in St Lou, Italy. Ruth and Martin had known one another in childhood. Over the years their paths parted, but had come together again through their handicaps.

Ruth's father wanted to buy her hand controls to put on a car so that she could drive. Knowing that Martin used a set, Mr. Graeff took Ruth to see Martin and his hand controls. With their friendship renewed, Martin and Ruth started going places together. In the last letter I had received from Ruth prior to making our visit, she had written that she and Martin were debating with her parents about getting married. Since Martin was an orphan, he had no parents to thrash out the pros and cons of two paraplegics' marrying. In addition to seeing Ruth and Martin in person for the first time, I was anxious to find out how their marriage discussions had worked themselves out.

Arriving in Lancaster, we found out that when Ruth went to see Martin, the visit had led to her winning Martin's heart as well as his hand controls. Ruth and Martin had married and returned to Lancaster from their honeymoon at the same time we arrived there. They spent their honeymoon in Niagara Falls, where Ruth's mother had accompanied them to help with Ruth's personal care. In addition to Martin's hand controls, Ruth also moved into Martin's house, which had been constructed to accommodate his wheelchair. The house had been built after Martin's injury. Prior to her marriage, Ruth had operated a manicure shop in the front room of her parent's home. After marriage, she closed shop and became a fulltime wife and housekeeper.

While I served as an example of the lack of treatment available for spinal injuries, Martin and Ruth were examples of paras receiving up-to-date therapy, especially Martin, who had the advantages of the Veterans Administration facilities.

Ruth and Martin could both slide into and out of a bed, car, or bathtub, and they could "jump" their small wheels on their chairs over slight obstacles, such as door sills and low curbings. While they were in process of demonstrating their skills to me, their front door bell rang. A salesman at the door casually glanced into the living room when the door was opened, and took another quick look when he saw three people in wheelchairs wheeling around inside the room. The salesman no doubt thought he had knocked on the door of a home for young cripples!

We left Lancaster with renewed determination at upgrading my rehabilitation. I was anxious to get back home and work on putting this new knowledge into practice. I did manage to get in and out of my hospital bed by myself. (Bill and I used matching hospital beds for sleeping.) But I never did master the technique of sliding into an automobile without someone to swing my knees and legs into the car. I did not accomplish as much as Ruth and Martin because my paralysis began at a much higher area of the body than theirs, which gives them an edge on overcoming their handicaps.

Soon after we arrived back home, Ruth, Martin, and the Graeffs wrote that they were coming to see us in Bessemer City while en route to Florida. When they arrived, Bill and I turned over our bedroom to Ruth and Martin so that they could use my built-in conveniences. During their visit, Bill and I slept in my former upstairs bedroom, where I had started my first days of paraplegia. The last time I had been in my "old" bedroom was after my marriage ceremony, when I changed my lace wedding gown for my going-away outfit. As Bill carried me up and down the stairs, we discussed the great number of happenings in our lives that had transpired since the last time he carried me down those steps as a new bride.

Lois and Lisa

18

Chapter Eighteen

As a paraplegic, I soon found out that traveling with a man at the wheel is not the same as riding with a female driver. Besides the convenience of his masculine strength, a man always gets me to my destination and back faster than the opposite sex. We women are prone to meander in whatever direction our whims take us, as long as we can keep veering back toward our goal. My most consistent chauffeur after I became paralyzed was a woman — my sister, Beatrice. When she was married on July 9, 1938, Mama and I had thought we had lost her forever. As a new bride, Beatrice kept house while her husband Carl attended Law School at Emory. However, before long she felt free to leave her husband at home with his law books, and make frequent visits with us, which enabled her to drive us around.

Beatrice excels at meandering while driving, which makes going places with her an unpredictable experience. As her passenger, I appreciated her impulsive traveling decisions but they exasperated my mother. I shared the sense of enjoyment Bea experienced behind the wheel. Trips with her were like a treasure hunt, as we meandered from place to place, slowly working our way to our intended destination.

For my first long trip as a cripple in the spring of 1939, Beatrice came home to take Mama and me on a week-long excursion. Joining us on our unknown destination was a mutual friend, Margaret Reid, and Mama's niece, Doris Jenkins, both from Lowell, North Carolina.

Bea was the only one with a husband, and he was busy studying for final exams. Not having any males around to try and keep us on course, we made a leisurely trip to the North Carolina and Virginia coasts, stopping whenever and wherever we fancied. Weighing less than ninety pounds, I was carried pack-saddle by Mama and Bea.

On that first trip, I learned that a handicapped person has to forget about dignity. Consequently, anything has been acceptable to me as long as it got me where I was going...even if, at times, my "bottom" did show. As a paraplegic being carried here and there by a variety of methods, I was "shooting the moon" thirty years before "mooning" became a fad in the '70's! Many times my bottom has been more prominently displayed than my face. But people are nice, they always look at the proper part of me, even if it is less interesting!

We made our first trip to the Outer Banks to see the third annual production of "The Lost Colony," and to visit the Kitty Hawk Memorial. I vaguely remember the outdoor drama and Wright Brothers' Memorial, but I vividly recall mountains of sand dunes and being bitten by a profusion of mosquitoes who let us know we were intruders in their bailiwick.

From the Outer Banks, we followed the coast to Virginia, stopping at every antique shop along the way, some of which we had to hunt for and find off the beaten path. I was pack-saddled inside the places of business, where I looked at everything but bought nothing. At that stage of paraplegia, I still had no promise of a future, and antiques are things to treasure as the years pass. In 1939, I asked myself, "How many years will I have to cherish such things?" Then, too, I thought, "If I spend money needlessly, how will I pay for my costly medical bills?"

Now I am not all that wise in money matters. My mother had a head for business and managed to emphasize the reality of my condition without making me feel depressed. The financial burden of a paraplegic is a knowledge I carry with me at all times.

As our all-female group continued our travels in a carefree

manner, my bowels grew carefree, too. I developed diarrhea. However, my condition was not embarrassing among the girls. I learned from that experience to consider such a situation just another handicap that I, as a paraplegic, have to endure from time to time. More importantly, I learned what and when to eat while traveling so that I never did suffer this predicament again.

We returned home with our car loaded with antiques and Virginia hams. Folks at home glanced at the antiques but devoured the sugar-cured hams, which had sweetened on our return to home base. The trip proved to me that a carload of females could travel together in harmony, and that, as a paraplegic, I could travel with others who were physically fit. That trip made me look forward to others.

After World War II, when my sister's family sold their home in Atlanta to move to Bessemer City, Beatrice continued to serve as our driver, taking Mama and me places, along with our first set of children, Bea's Tommy and Bobby, and my Sammy and Annette. Traveling with three adults and four children, our trips never operated on an even keel.

Our offspring kept upsetting the auto-cart!

The trip we seven made to Raleigh proved one to remember. Bea's husband was elected to serve a term as a State Representative in Raleigh. Through Carl's efforts, the children were named Honorary Pages to the general assembly. To make the event more meaningful, we made a trip to the state Capitol, so that the four youngsters could receive their honor at the scene of government action. This was a mistake.

It turned out that as far as the children were concerned, they would have been more thrilled to stay home and watch reruns of home movies. We adults would have fared better, too, if we had let the children receive their page certificates from the mailman.

Being at their friskiest stage, our offspring were not the least bit thrilled at the prospect of making a trip to the North Carolina State Capitol.

When we did arrive at the imposing structure, the only thing about it that struck a chord of interest for the youngsters was the statues placed here and there outside the building. During our brief visit to the General Assembly session, the boys kept leaving the legislature proceedings to dart outside and climb onto historical figures from the past. This resulted in Mama and Bea having to rush after them numerous times and drag them off their statuary scalings.

With this honorary business completed, we discarded our previous plan to show off other seats of government to our little scholars. We realized our efforts would not be appreciated.

By the end of the day, our spirits were sagging, and we were more than eager to return to the haven of our home. Before leaving Raleigh, Bea did make a stop at a chain grocery store to buy food to ward off hunger pains and keep the children busy eating. They bickered over who had the outside window seats, which were, according to them, the most prestigious positions.

"My time....my time," became their shouting cry as they raced for the choice seats.

Arriving at the grocery store, the children scrambled into the building, tagging along with Beatrice. After completing her purchases, Bea came back to the car where Mama helped her to reload our evasive young passengers, who at times were more hectic than Bea's and my childhood efforts to catch chickens for Sunday dinner. With the children all finally seated and busy eating, we headed for home.

Just as Bea swung into traffic, Bobby excitedly asked, "Where's Sammy?" Each head inside our car turned to search for Sammy. But Sammy was not in the car. My mind went as paralyzed as my legs. I could not imagine how Sammy could have disappeared into thin air. Had he been with us, I frantically thought, when we left the Capitol? This was a distinct possibility since loading my chair and me into a car always created confusion.

Loading all the children at the same time could prove maddening. Mama and Bea, who were maintaining their sanity, theorized that the only place Sammy could possibly be was the grocery store. In order to return there to conduct a search, Bea made an illegal u-turn and retraced the exact route she had taken from the store. As we waited outside the grocery store, it seemed no time before we saw Bea coming back to the car followed by Sammy. She had found him just inside the front entrance where he was absorbed in latching and unlatching the chain that kept customers in line.

That chain really worked for the new Honorary Page. It kept Sammy in line over-time.

The first time Sammy got lost, I was not on the scene to panic. Again he was with his Aunt Beatrice. Some cousins the same age as our children had come from Louisiana for a visit, and Bea had taken them, along with our four children, for a tour of Charlotte.

I had remained at home for this excursion. Sammy, who was eight years old and into space travel, left home dressed for the grand jaunt wearing a beanie cap equipped with a pinwheel on top, which revolved in the wind as he walked along carrying space comic books.

The children left for Charlotte as keyed up with excitement as if they were on their way to the circus. Before noon, they had already lost their vigor after seeing historical sites, and by the time Beatrice ended the tour in the late afternoon at Ivey's Department Store in downtown Charlotte, they had grown contrary and hungry.

They became more so the longer they stayed at Ivey's. Bea not only meanders as a driver, she ambles as a shopper, and is never in a hurry to make her purchases. The family group was in the Little Girls Dresses section when the lights blinked to signal store closing time. Bea ignored their blinking as she was not ready to leave. Annette had asked her dotin' aunt, "Take me where the pretty dresses are." Since Annette was the only girl in our family and among our friends, she was the Little Princess who always got her wishes fulfilled. Bea, fulfilling the Little Princess's wish, was still looking at the "the pretty dresses" when she and her companions were pushed out the front door -- but not before Beatrice had purchased a dress for Annette to start the first grade in.

From Ivey's, the group walked to the S & W Cafeteria for their evening meal. As they were seated, they split up into two groups. Bobby Howard passed chewing gum around to the younger ones. When he looked for his cousin Sammy to give him his stick of gum, Sammy was not there.

This time, Bea panicked and became petrified at the possibility that Sammy could have been locked inside of Ivey's. She rushed to a telephone to call the Charlotte Police Department and report a lost eight-year-old boy. The sergeant at the desk, hearing her problem, said, "Calm down, Lady. we'll hook-up with a patrol car," and radioed, "Come in Car No. 102."

Car No. 102 reported in, and the sergeant asked, "You still have that little boy?" Car No. 102 answered that it did indeed still have a little boy in custody. The patrolman was instructed to take the lost child to the S & W for identification. Beatrice and her tour group were anxiously waiting on the sidewalk in front of the cafeteria when the patrol car rolled to a stop.

In the back seat sat a little boy wearing a beanie cap with a pinwheel revolving on top. It was Sammy. As he was reunited with family members, Sammy was quite proud at being the center of attention. In explaining how he came to be riding in a patrol car, Sammy said when several of their group walked out of the store before his Aunt Beatrice, he went with them to the front entrance where benches were provided for shoppers. Sammy said, "I sat down to read my book. When I looked up, everybody was gone." He walked out onto the sidewalk but, "I did not see anyone I knew," he said. Sammy found his way to the parking lot where the car had once been and the attendant there turned him over to police.

When Bea and her entourage returned home later than expected, Annette rushed in to make the first report to me, saying with agitation, "We lost Sammy in Charlotte." Before she could relate the entire story, I burst into tears. As I started to cry, my son came strolling into my room. Not looking in my direction, he walked straight to my telephone, picked it up, and said, "Calling Car No. 102."

Being lost had been a thrill for my only son, and in turn made him the envy of his cousins, especially for his familiarity with the operations of Car No. 102.

For some child-losing, I have to take full blame. One afternoon shortly after Lisa was born, I loaded the car with youngsters to drive them to the Ramseur farm in the country. My young passengers were filled with anticipation and talked over the loud radio's music, planning what they all would do when they got there. They talked about skipping rocks in the creek, hunting eggs, and more. In the midst of their youthful chattering, and the radio playing almost as loud as their voices, their spirits flying high as we rode along, suddenly 12-year-old Annette gasped as she said in alarm, "We left Lisa!" With a start, I realized we had indeed left Lisa in an empty house.

We returned home in good speed, and the second the car turned into the driveway, Annette leaped out of the car and raced upstairs to my former bedroom, now called "Annette's bedroom." There she found Lisa lying in the middle of a twin bed, gazing at her surroundings and unaware that she had been the sole mistress of her dominion for thirty minutes. After twelve years without looking after an infant, I kept forgetting I had Lisa!

On the last long trip we made with Beatrice as the driver, we still had the same traveling crew of Howards, Smiths, and Sexton. Neither Lisa nor Bea's James David had been born. When

Bea and I reached the milestone of having three children each, we outgrew traveling together in one car.

By the time Lisa and James David arrived, our older children were teenagers, and went their separate ways. We parents went ours while the two babies stayed home. For our "last trip" with Bea as driver, we went to Florida. Heading South, we took a swing West to visit with my Agnes Scott roommate, Anita Howard Perry, who lived in Nashville, Georgia. Like me, Anita had married her hometown sweetheart, Bill Perry. At the time of our visit, Anita had three children: Sarah Amelia, and "Little" Bill. Her Steve came later in life, like Lisa.

Several summers before, Anita and her two older children had visited Bea and me in Bessemer City. Our visit, we told her, was meant to pay her back! When Anita, her two children, and her maid came for their visit, the Howard boys moved in with the Smith children and each brought along a friend. Regulating the children soon became like overseeing a correction home for juvenile delinquents, with each of them displaying a tendency for misbehaving. Anita's family visit with us in North Carolina had been rough. Our return trip to Nashville was rougher.

This excursion to Nashville was not the first time Bea and I had taken off for the South Georgia town, but it was the first time we made it all the way there. On our initial failed attempt to reach Nashville, Anita was getting married to a young man from Athens, Georgia, and Bea and I were on our way to her wedding. We never made it. A telegram stopped us in Atlanta. It stated, "Don't come. I have married Bill Perry." Everything was ready for Anita's wedding but Anita. The flowers were ordered, the bridesmaids with their bridal dresses had arrived, gifts were coming in. Then at the last hour, Anita decided Bill Perry was the man she loved -- so she married him in a small ceremony instead of the large church affair she had planned with her Athens fiance.

Anita, in later years, says she has never regretted having the nerve to call off her scheduled wedding, even if she waited until the eleventh hour.

When Bea, Mama, the children, and I arrived in Nashville, the children started a high tempo of activity while the older ones stayed idle with exhaustion. When we North Carolinians brought our visit in Nashville to a close, Sammy was wearing high heel cowboy boots that I had bought from Little Bill.

Sammy had fallen in love with the boots Bill had outgrown. After we loaded our luggage and children to continue on our way to Florida, we left Little Bill richer and his mother limp. While we loaded the car, Anita was lying on a porch swing, breaking out with hives. She had a medical appointment scheduled for later that day. She scratched with one hand and waved her goodbyes with the other from her prone position as we drove out of her driveway.

With our children bursting with energy, and envy over Sammy's Cowboy boot-buy, we left Georgia for Silver Springs, Florida, stopping only for gas and snacks. We arrived in Silver Springs in the late afternoon and went straight to the amusement area of the springs before we looked for a motel for the night. I stayed in the car while Mama and Beatrice channeled four children in the direction of the entrance. My respite was short. In no time, Mama and Bea came back seeming highly agitated and the children looking disappointed, except for Sammy who was high-stepping in his cowboy boots.

The reason for the quick return was that, when Mama opened her pocket book to pay for admission, all her folding money was gone, vanished in mid-air. That meant all of our money was gone since Mama handled all of the money to finance our trip.

We found ourselves hundreds of miles from home, one paraplegic, two tired adults, and four children, all of us hungry, with no money -- and dusk falling fast. While Bea and Mama were frantically looking through Esso Credit slips to find the names of the gas stations where we had stopped, Sammy came prancing up in his boots with his hands stuck inside his tight cowboy pants pockets. He pulled both hands out of his pockets at the same time, and bills, real money bills, scattered in all directions.

Sammy asked, "Is this the money you are talking about?" It was! Mama and Bea scurried to pick up the money. This time, Mama pinned her money to her bra for safe keeping.

Later, Mama asked Sammy, "How did you get Mama Anne's money?!?" He told her, "When you were sleeping, I looked in your pocket book and saw the money and I put it all in my pockets!" Silently, I prayed that this habit of taking money that did not belong to him would not develop into a permanent trait. My prayers were answered. Sammy would now make a high mark in an honesty test given by Diogenes.

Lois, Bill, and Sammy

Lois and Bill

19

Chapter Nineteen

That first day in 1947 when my husband set my paralyzed bottom in the driver's seat of our car, and I placed one hand on the steering knob and the other on the hand control lever, I realized I had found a new home in my car.

I started rolling along the roads twice as much as I rolled my wheelchair on the floor at home. I was approaching thirty, but acting as bad as a sixteen-year-old boy who just got his first driver's license. I began cranking up my car to drive just to be driving.

Driving put an upswing in my activities, broadened the scope of my environment, and ran up my gasoline bill. It also made me feel as though I was becoming my own master in deciding which route to follow.

Driving my first time using hand controls, my husband, whose temperament is geared to take off faster than a race car, was my first passenger and doubled as my driving instructor. To our amazement, we both passed the trial run. Bill kept his nerves in check, and I kept the car on the road. Passing my first driver's license test as a paraplegic turned out to be as easy as driving with hand controls. I was the first para the examiner had ever taken out for a road test,and he was as eager as I was to get it all over with.

He did not make my driving drills last any longer than he had to. That examiner passed me driving on the first round, because I don't think he wanted me to take him out onto the highway for a second spin around.

There was one thing that did worry me about driving with my

first set of hand controls. It was the vacuum-type brakes which braked faster than regular brakes. I had visions of someone ramming into the rear end of my car, as my brakes slammed to a quick stop. Using my intuition to work out problems, I copied the wording that was used on tractor-trailers before power brakes became standard equipment. Like those truckers, I had the words printed onto the trunk of the car, "Caution. Air Brakes." My idea did not produce the results I had expected. Instead of drivers keeping their wary distance, they tailgated me in order to read my printed message and to gawk at me. In addition to arousing the curiosity of my fellow road travelers, my warning also provided wit for my peers, mainly my husband, who (with a bit of male chauvinism), pointed out, "You would get better results if you had put the words, 'Woman At The Wheel.'"

Using only two hands to drive instead of two hands and two feet, I should have had a passenger deficiency, but I didn't. I soon found myself operating a popular but profitless transit system. One person I could always count on to hop in the car when I slid behind the wheel was my mother, who had never developed the knack for driving.

In her case, ignorance made her a sublime passenger. She did not know enough about driving to experience any apprehension or uneasiness riding with me. My children and their friends were as complacent as my mother. Like her, the children did not care who did the driving, as long as they got to go, and with me as the driver, we did a lot of going.

Eventually, driving became both a chore and a pleasure when I found myself serving as chauffeur to my children, madly driving them here and there. I wore out more auto tires than I did wheelchair tires.

Being able to drive my children but not being able to get out of the car to accompany them inside different places made them more self-sufficient at an early age, I believe. When I drove them as youngsters to a doctor's or dentist's office, they never balked at having to go in by themselves for treatments and examinations -- until they became older and took themselves. Then they started moaning and groaning as they kept their medical appointments.

I got a kick out of Lisa when she was a toddler. After calling her doctor's office, I would drive to the back door of his office building and let Lisa out of the car, and she would run toward the door where a nurse opened it to let her in. Lisa toddled in, holding out a finger to be pricked for her blood test. When the children were growing up, I charged at one drug store in town and paid cash at the other. If I handed a note to Lisa to go for ice cream, without saying a word, she toddled to the drug store where I charged. If I handed her money, without saying a word to her, she went running toward the drug store where I paid cash.

Like the nurses at the doctor's office and the clerks at the stores, whenever I needed help driving my children or myself places, my family members, friends, and even strangers were always willing helpers. Bill had told me about a four-year-old boy, the same age as Sammy, being able to walk to town by himself to get purchases and pay for them. I thought, "Why can't Sammy do the same?" since we lived near the business area.

I sent Sammy off walking to town with money and instructions. In no time, a man came carrying Sammy on his shoulders up to our front door. The man said, "Mrs. Smith, I found your little boy walking on main street by himself -- so I brought him home because I knew you would worry when you missed him."

I thanked him and decided to wait until Sammy became a little older before making him my errand boy.

Another instance help came my way stands out in my memory. It occurred when Sammy was an infant and before Bill returned with his Air Force discharge from India. I took Sammy along with a group of females to a Gastonia theatre to see a movie. A dwarf employed there at the picture show always gave me special attention by opening doors and finding outside aisle seats. When we drove up to the movie entrance, seeing me, the midget rushed out to the car to open the door. Seeing nothing but females inside the car, he said to me, "I'll get my brother to carry you. He works here, too." My dubious fears about a dwarf's brother being able to carry me disappeared when the brother walked up, six feet tall. With the brother carrying me and the dwarf carrying Sammy, we created an unusual scene for downtown Gastonians to stare at. The dwarf's smile was as broad as he was tall at being the first one to carry Sammy inside to sleep through his first movie.

I found out driving myself helped me gathering news, especially when I freelanced and served as stringer for several daily newspapers. As a driver I could take off after any siren and find out what it was and what had made it sound off. Annette now claims me being an ambulance, fire truck, and police car chaser when she was young made her feel insecure, mainly when she helped me shop.

My shopping was done small-town style, where everyone knows each other. At times, I made a want list and called it in, then picked up my order later with one of my children running in for my purchases. Or I made a list and one of the children ran it into the store while I parked outside the entrance. I could yell information concerning my list. And when Annette took my weekly list into the grocery store, the grocer stepped to the door and called to me, "Mrs. Smith, did you want anything else besides bubble gum?"

If I was sitting outside waiting for my youthful shoppers to return with my purchases and a fire truck or anything else that looked newsworthy passed along, I would take off after it. After getting the details, I would then drive back to pick up my little carrying aide. Annette, recalling my enthusiasm for running down news, says, "Coming out of a store and not finding my mother waiting for me in the car always gave me a deserted feeling!"

Lisa made sure she would not be abandoned when I sent her into stores to do my bidding. She would not budge from the car until I handed her my car keys.

Being able to drive turned me into a newspaper carrier. When Sammy took on a morning route, I took on the job with him. I started making the rounds to customers on cold, rainy mornings, which eventually turned into an everyday event. In addition to his dog, Lucky, accompanying us, Sammy's friends and their dogs joined our group. Feeling she was missing out on the fun, Annette plus a girlfriend soon joined the troupe. Before long, my station wagon was filled with girls, boys, dogs, and newspapers. This entourage made for problems during the dawn deliveries.

When Lucky and the other canines accompanying us trespassed into some other dog's residential territory, dog fights erupted. Along with dog fights, the carriers shouted at one another in gay spirits, as they ran and threw papers at the customer's houses. Before long, fights between girls and boys developed. The sounds of dog snarls, youthful shouts, and bickering did not please customers who were not early risers, especially the ones who worked second shifts or were late sleepers on Sunday mornings. To the relief of Sammy's customers (and me), the then weekly paper soon folded after its inception.

I will never forget the sight-seeing trip Mama and I made with the four children the Thanksgiving holidays before my Lisa and Bea's James David were born. Mama and I took my Sammy and Annette and Bea's Tommy and Bobby to Florida with plans to arrive on Thanksgiving Day at the home of Aunt Ede and Uncle Joe Rothman, who had retired to live in Lake Placid, Florida. As we traveled en route to Lake Placid, I filmed the children on 16mm film as they looked at different tourist attractions, mostly snakes and alligators.

Headed toward Marineland, we noticed the car in front of us make a quick stop and pull off to the side of the road. The driver hopped out of his car and started searching intently through the roadside weeds. Out of curiosity, several cars stopped. Our car was among them. We found out the man was looking for a Diamondback Rattler he had run over. The snake had crawled into the weeds to die there in the undergrowth. Tommy, looking at the dead snake, thought of all the possible uses he could make of it. He had joined a boy scout troop and had visions of taking the snake's rattlers, and maybe its hide, back to show off to his scout friends.

He started begging Mama and me to let him take the dead snake to Aunt Ede's, where he said he would dress it that night. Mama did not cater to her eldest grandson's plans one whit, but spineless me, I relented to Tommy's pleas and told him we would take the snake. "We can put it in our lunch box," I said to my youthful tourists, "Oh no, we won't," my mother quickly objected. "I am not riding with a dead snake at my feet!" This she said with finality.

Tommy, not wanting to leave a treasure lying in Florida weeds, asked, "Why can't I cram it into the rear bumper?" I thought the rear bumper would make the ideal carrying rack for a dead Florida Diamondback Rattler, and indeed it did. The snake fit perfectly, extending from one tail light to the other. Before Tommy packed his rattler inside the bumper, I took movie shots of him picking the dead rattler up from the ground. Always the showman, Tommy eagerly posed with the rattler draped around his neck. The other children clamored to have their picture taken as snake-handlers. They passed the rattler around, taking turns holding it while I recorded their performance on film for posterity. That rattler was long and as thick as my forearm, I noted.

We arrived at Marineland with children and snake intact. While Mama dutifully ushered the kids inside to see the exhibits, I wrote postcards in the parking lot to friends back home as

I waited, telling them about our trip and about our rattlesnake find. While writing, I started thinking about the dead snake. I breathlessly thought, if it were alive, "It could crawl into this car through the station wagon's open tailgate window." And if it did, I frantically realized, I had no way of getting out of its path. While I was thinking these thoughts, Mama came back to the car. I said to her "Mama, check to see if that snake is really dead."

She made an inspection of the rear bumper and came back to report, "That snake is lifeless." While the children were looking at leaping dolphins, Mama thought she and I should get our gas tank filled. We drove to a nearby gas station we had noticed near Marineland. As the attendant put gas in our tank, I hoped he would not notice our dead snake. He didn't. When we returned to the parking lot, I still had an uneasy feeling about that snake.

I said, "Mama, would you check on that snake again?" Feeling a little exasperated at me, Mama reluctantly walked to the back of the car to make her second inspection and verify the snake was indeed dead. As she started around the back of the car, the dead rattler reared its head and hissed at Mama. Mama screamed. I almost jumped out of my skin. The snake was not dead. It had only been stunned and the hot fumes from the exhaust had brought it back to life, fighting mad.

With the rattler in the car bumper, I was terrified. The children came back to the car at the same time the snake hissed and struck at Mama, and huddled together at a safe distance, leaving me in the car alone with the snake. I pulled myself up out of the driver's seat to look toward the rear of the station wagon, expecting any minute for the infuriated rattler to charge me. That deadly poisonous snake at my back made me nearly keyed up enough to perform a "take up thy bed and walk" miracle.

Fortunately, Tommy had crammed the snake inside the bumper in such a way that the only portion of its body it could move was its head, which the snake bobbed up and down in striking motions. As the snake hissed and moved its head, we were a helpless bunch, an aged female, a crippled female, and four scared-to-death youngsters, alone in the parking lot!

And, not a one of us a match for the invigorated, born-again rattler.

Tommy and Sammy were sent to find help at the service station where Mama and I had bought gas. A station attendant with a tire iron in hand came to deliver us from our Diamondback. He used the tool to strike at the snake's head as it hissed from its bumper prison. Our rescuer, just as edgy as his audience, kept hitting at the snake's bobbin' head. He nervously told us about the different people he had known who had died from rattler bites. His narration intensified our frenzied emotions, and we unanimously hoped this snake fight would end in favor of us humans.

From out of nowhere, it seemed, a crowd gathered. None of us travelers had the nerve to tell the inquisitive how the large rattler had gotten into our bumper. We let them assume it had crawled inside of its own free will.

When the snake was finally decapitated, the attendant cautiously removed its remains from the bumper and buried the dead-once-again snake for a price which Mama and I gladly paid.

Numerous times I've thought about the "if's" of our rattlesnake adventure. I have these tormenting pictures of Tommy posing with it dangling around his neck, and the children passing it around to one another, as though they were playing a parlor game while I filmed. If my memory gets hazy, I can refresh it with the home movies. I also cringe over the thoughts of the gas attendant placing the gasoline's nozzle at the tank opening, located just above the "dead" rattler's head.

The snake event did not shake-up the children as it did me. As we traveled home, the only places they wanted to make stops were alligator and snake farms. Tommy did manage to bring home rattlers -- ones we bought, along with a treated rattler's head, which exposed its fangs. I could not appreciate Tommy's purchases in the same manner he and the other children did.

As we drove homeward, I ignored Tommy sitting beside me as he entertained his comrades by pretending he was picking his teeth with the rattler's fangs. At this stage of life, I was well practiced in the art of ignoring human beings — but not live Diamondback Rattlers!

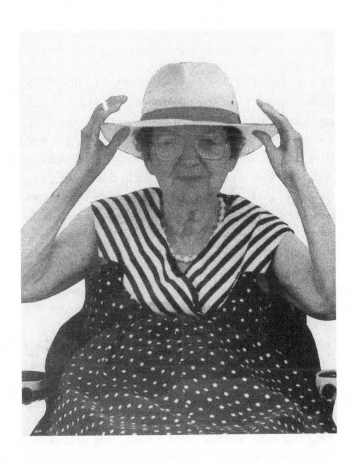

Lois

20

Chapter Twenty

During the early years of my paraplegia when I enjoyed a childlike way of never looking full-face at reality, I indulged in being a fantasist. As most females probably do, I fantasized about my physical condition, picturing myself as a normal, attractive person, and when I let my imagination run rampant, I thought of "Glamorous Me." Nothing destroyed this glamour image faster than a look in a mirror, which forced me to face the reality of my handicaps. Growing up, Lisa must have shared these early fantasies about my appearance. Among her elementary school papers, I found a crayon drawing of a normal looking woman. It was captioned, "My Dear Mother." On another piece of paper, she had drawn a stringy-headed woman sitting in a run-down wheelchair. Under it she had written, "My Own Dear Mother."

The same year Annette won the title of "Miss Bessemer City," I received the North Carolina Handicapped Worker of the Year Award for 1967. En route home from Raleigh, where Governor Dan Moore presented the award, we parked by the sidewalk in a small town. A group of girls walked in front of our car, not looking our way, as they went by laughing and talking. Lisa, filled with the glamour of our titles, smirkingly remarked to Annette, "They don't know Miss North Carolina Handicap is in this car!" Congratulations did come my way, but no one ever clamored around my chair begging for my autograph.

Later, Lisa made efforts to find some upsides to me being older than her friends' mothers. As my youngest child, Lisa was very much aware that I was closer to the ages of her friends' grandmothers than their mothers. One day she brought a group of friends home. Their mothers were following the trend of wearing hot pants and knee boots while I wore full skirts and bootees.

Lisa took a staunch stand of defense by my wheelchair and, trying to produce something super about me, nonchalantly remarked, "My mother is forty-six years old, and she still has her own teeth." I do not know if this information scored with her friends, but it left me feeling like Red Riding Hood's Grandmother.

In spite of my stringy hair, run-down wheelchair, and lack of dental plates, I rarely sensed a feeling of being excluded from the activities of my family and friends. After I was injured, several girlfriends asked me to serve as a bridesmaid for their weddings, which I did. To participate in the weddings, my usher-partner carried me down the church aisle with him in his formals and me in bridesmaid dress, carrying a bouquet.

My position was usually on the front pew next to the parents of the bride. Following the ceremony, the same usher plucked me in his arms and briskly carried me back down the aisle with the other usher-escorted bridesmaids for the recessional. During one wedding, and a big formal one at that, I played the piano for the bride's entry, the recessional, and the Just Married couple. My piano playing probably created more attention than the bride's wedding gown.

Mendelssohn's "Wedding March" never sounded tin-pannie until I played it for my friend's wedding, and all without the benefit of the piano pedal. At that time, I had a chair with small wheels, which I sat in while others did the rolling. For my turn at the piano, someone pushed my chair in front of the keyboard. As I struck the resounding chords that heralded the bride's entry, each one of my ten fingers trembled as though trying to set a record for shaking. Producing quick, jerky sounds and disjointed notes, I was more nervous than the bridegroom as I played most females' favorite tune.

I hope the couple's married life has not been as discordant as their wedding march sounded!

When Sammy arrived, he upstaged me in more ways than one. He took my place in my friends' weddings. During one month of June, Sammy served as ring bearer in three weddings. He became confused going to so many rehearsals, weddings, and parties, and frequently asked, "Now who is it I am marrying this time?"

When I join my family and friends in activities, I do not feel as though I am a freak. It could be mind over matter, but in approaching life, I do not feel I am different to any great degree from others. My family shares this image of me as a person -- a whole person, not a broken one.

After over thirty-five years of marriage, when my husband calls me, he says, "Lossie, walk in here a minute...." Bill knew me before I became wheelchair bound, and says when he is away from me he does not have a mental picture of me as an invalid. My children have never known me as anything other than a handicapped person. But like their father, they too say they do not carry a mental image of me as an invalid mother.

When Lisa assisted Annette in producing a United Way television documentary, she set up the filming of handicapped and disadvantaged people. Lisa told me, "I felt depressed seeing the handicapped people. I almost cried, I felt so sorry for them." She smiled as she added, "But then I realized that none of the handicapped people we were filming was as severely handicapped as you and, all at once, it hit me that I had never thought of you as being someone to feel sorry for."

Others knowing me as a cripple but treating me like a normal person enabled me to participate in activities that might otherwise have been off-limits to a paraplegic. After becoming a paraplegic, I not only served as a bridesmaid and wedding pianist for the first time, but I also rode in my first motor boat, went sailing, and took my first airplane flight. In the summer of 1940, Mike Goldberg turned over his boat keys to our group, but mostly to me. He owned an inboard with a hand throttle that I could operate all by myself. It gave me a big thrill to be at the boat wheel and be the one to zip along the Catawba River.

One day while I was at the wheel of the boat, our boat met up in mid-stream with a sailboat, the only one on the river that day. Making conversation with the sailor, I was invited to sail with him. While the sail boat owner, a Springs from Fort Mill, South Carolina, held the boats, Jimmy Ritter picked me up and sat me on the sailboat's floorboard, and I sailed for the first and last time. I never had the chance to sail again until Sammy built his own sailboat but by that time, I had lost most of my adventuresome spirit.

When Sammy got his pilot's license, it was not my lack of spirit that kept me from flying with him. It was my memory of Sammy getting lost over an airport in Pittsburgh, caught by darkness and getting low on fuel while piloting his mother-in-law for the first time. I did not want to chance sharing the same experience as Mrs. Stuart B. Babbage.

Even when I was younger, I had mixed feelings of fear and delight about flying. Pinckney Stowe owned a four-seater plane and when we flew in it and "buzzed" Bessemer City, I was always afraid to lean over and look down at my hometown or wave to Mama and others who stood waving skyward from our yard. I clung to the notion that if I leaned over, it would tilt the plane, and I did not want the plane to tilt while I was in it.

I feel the same way on commercial planes. Window seats are wasted on me. In flight, I keep my face and nose facing forward. I never relax, but sit there like a statue, never looking right or left.

I act the same way when I am a passenger in a car. I rarely take my eyes off the road. Even with seat belts, I still maintain a sharp look-out, as though I was riding shotgun for a stagecoach driver. Being in several auto accidents has made me edgy.

Among the other "firsts" that happened after I became a para was riding on a motorcycle, joining a sorority, and being in my first parade. The motorcycle ride came about when Jimmy Ritter and Jerry Wyatt made their home with us that one year. One summer evening, they took me for a spin on their motorcycle. Jerry sat me behind Jimmy, who roared us around a city block. It was fun having the wind and bugs hitting my face, but I was terrified of every inch of that block. I would never recommend motorcycle riding for paras.

Later, I agonized over the "ifs." What if reflex action had caused my foot to become caught in a wheel? What if I had let loose of my tight hold on Jimmy's waist and I had flopped over backwards like a rag doll? After thinking such thoughts, I decided to never ride double on a motorcycle or bicycle again.

Since Agnes Scott did not have national social sororities, I had never had the chance to join one. After I became crippled, I was invited to be a charter member of the Gastonia Chapter of Delta Theta Chi, a non-collegiate sorority. Excepting myself, membership must have been regulated by good looks; the sorority popped with pretty faces. These pretty faces worked to my advantage because I never lacked for a male carrier to take me to weekly meetings held at the Arlington Hotel in Gastonia. My sorority meeting carriers were almost always Billy Gamble and Buddy Mauney. Both looked forward to mingling with attractive girls as the only males in the crowd.

Two events stand out for me about my sorority days -- a trip to Winston-Salem, North Carolina, and being in my first parade.

I made the trip to Winston-Salem to see the annual Moravian Easter Sunrise service. Since our Easter Sunrise service ceremony hails from Moravian tradition, I had always wanted to attend one. When my first chance arrived, I experienced mixed emotions. On the morning our sorority was to leave for Winston-Salem, Bill called to say he was home on furlough, arriving earlier than expected. I wanted to be with him and I wanted to make the trip. I was truly a cripple up Cripple Creek, trying to make my decision.

I had offered to take others in my car to Winston-Salem, and I kept my pledge. When my car took off for Easter weekend, I was in it. Prior to going, I held reservations about how I, as an arm-carried invalid, would fare at such an event. My worries were needless, as the ceremony is all sound, and can be heard over most of the city. Starting at 2 a.m. on Easter Sunday, Moravian bands in buses cover the city playing Easter music. As the sun starts to rise, the bands and sunrise-service-goers gather in the Moravian graveyard, where a brief service is held as the minister shouts, "Christ The Lord Has Risen Today!" and those gathered, shout back, "He has Risen Indeed!" Then the bands play together as the sun rises higher.

The sun had not risen too high before we were high-tailing it for home. As soon as I was carried in the house, I called Bill to tell him, "I'm back!" Since I came back earlier than Bill had expected, he still uses this incident to say, "Lossie chased after me." Me, chasing him, when I could not even walk?

My parade adventure came about thanks to cotton. Before synthetics started rolling off mill rollers to make more bolts of cloth than cotton did, cotton was still King of the South in 1940-41. At that time Gaston County prided itself at being the "Combed Yarn Center of the World." To brag, Gastonia Jaycees staged several cotton parades, which were almost like a mini Mardi Gras. A King Cotton was selected along with a Queen of Cotton. The parade was followed by a ball.

Our sorority sponsored a float, which I helped assemble for one of the parades. Using props belonging to me, we made a double entry, featuring one float for "Then" and one float for "Now." The "Then" entry was my surrey, without a "fringe on top," with Tommie Hazelton and me sitting on the back seat, dressed as Southern plantation ladies in fancy bonnets and long, ruffled dresses. The surrey was driven by a black driver dressed in top hat, black suit, white shirt, and black tie. Sitting beside him was three-year-old blonde, curly-headed Shirley Whitley, dressed in a small-fry Southern plantation era style. With her blonde ringlets, she could have served as a double for Shirley Temple. We looked like a scene from the movie, Mister Bojangles.

Directly behind the surrey was the "Now" theme, featuring my black Buick phaeton with the top down, the backs of the seats and fenders covered with sorority sisters dressed in stylish current-day sports wear. The "sisters" exposed a lot of leg, which added to our float's overall appeal.

I headed the sorority parade project, securing driver and horse, and making sure the surrey made the seven miles to Gastonia and back. I have no idea how I worked these details out because the parade itself was the first time my horse had been hitched to my surrey while I owned it.

My Uncle Gus Phifer found the surrey in Hickory, North Carolina, and bought it for me for a song. I do not remember how the ole-timey conveyance was transported to Bessemer City. While I owned it, the surrey had to sit outside in all manner of weather, which made Mama and me decide to sell it. We sold my surrey for a "bigger song" than we had bought it -- five dollars! I cannot recall to whom we sold it or how it was delivered to its new owner.

After marriage, sorority activities and youthful types of pleasure gradually became things of the past for me; my interest focused more and more on my husband, children, and career. Much to my surprise and my husband's delight, along the way, I eventually turned out to be a good cook. I do not brag about it as cooking to me is a necessity, not a hobby. I did bake once for a Gaston County Fair and won first place on all my entries, including Best Decorated Cake. My decorated cake was inspected but not sampled, which pleased me since I had used more of a bread dough than cake mixture for my lamb-shaped entry. I will admit I received more satisfaction over the money I won than I did proving that I could bake "best."

One time the Gastonia Gazette featured me as a cook along with printing my favorite recipes. The article was captioned, "She Likes To Cook But Likes Talking More!" Given a choice, I'd rather talk -- or write -- than cook.

I confess I kept staying on the community action list because it took me almost forty years to learn to say the word "No" and stick to it. I realized that I could do community and church work only because other people helped me. Now nearing sixty years of age and running out of nerve and steam, I have slowed down almost to a stall when it comes to doing outside of my home and my career. I've lost some of my nerve as I find myself running out of "oomph" and having the audacity to ask others for assistance.

The culmination of my handicapped years have dimmed both my "oomph" and conceit. Growing nearer to a sixtieth birthday also does something to one's Push and Shove. All at once, I have become aware that most of my "pushing and shoving" is now directed toward producing my own "get up and go". It takes most of my energy now to keep myself in drive instead of park.

As a working mother and housekeeper, I found after age fifty-five there is a big difference in what needs to be pushed. Gradually the truth hit me that my interests now revolve more and more around my health. Until age fifty my health was something that was always there. All at once, it is the only thing there, and life is now consumed with daily pill-taking, looking after my eliminations, warding off pressure sores, and trying to remember what I have said to whom. It is no use denying it. With age, bowel movements replace sex as bedroom talk. My husband never asks me any more, "How is your love life?" He asks instead, "How was your bowel movement today?" And I knew I had reached the Golden Years when my husband gave me a stainless steel bed pan for our thirty-fifth wedding anniversary, and I appreciated it!

One thing that has stayed with me through the years is my sense of humor. I manage to find things in life that help me laugh my miseries away. With all my new and old handicaps, I am still discovering that a paraplegic can keep laughter in her life, even as she ages into being a Senior Citizen.

I confess, I did not go rolling through my handicap years laughing all the time. Being a cripple is nothing to laugh about. I wasn't doing much laughing when I was an eighteen-year-old teenager in those first days as a paraplegic and was lying in my upstairs bedroom at night with my windows raised. I could hear the sounds of the night coming through the window, hearing the laughter of young people as they rode by in automobiles or walked by the house. Hearing their youthful, happy laughter made me wonder if happiness had gone from my life forever.

I owe it to God that through His mercy, kindness, and compassion, He provided me with a family and friends who were able to help bring laughter back to my life. I may have ridden out my forty years on the pity of others, but I did it laughing most of the way, with the joy of knowing that I had been truly blessed. With my husband, children, and grandchildren, with my relatives and friends, plus a successful career, what more could I have asked for? If I had not been an invalid, would I have ever found out the sterling qualities of my husband, family, and friends?

I look back at the extraordinary life I have led, and wonder about the walking woman I could have been. Would I relish the freedom to move, to lead a full life, or would I drift through life's ordinary experiences as just another aging housewife? Would I discover my life's true friend and weapon, the bittersweet tears of laughter?

Lisa, Sammy and Annette

Afterward

Mama's remarkable life story ended in a car wreck. Thanksgiving weekend, 1994, as she wastraveling home from spending the holiday with my family at Pawleys Island, SC., her handicap van driver, a dear friend of the family, ran a red light obscured by the setting sun. Mama died instantly.

After all that Mama had been through, I kept thinking this can't be. How could Mama survive a near fatal wreck as a teenager but perish in a wreck years after becoming a Grandmother?

Her death was devastating to our families, her grandchildren, her friends, and her town of Bessemer City, NC. She was a lively, vibrant person even in her old age. She enjoyed people and people enjoyed her. Flags flew at half-staff until sunrise on the day of her funeral, November 30, 1994.

She led a remarkable life, and was publicly recognized for her many achievements. She was inducted into the Order of the Long Leaf Pine Society, North Carolina's highest civilian award, by Governor James B Hunt, Jr. Her hometown celebrated Lois Smith Day in March, 1994, and she was givenmany awards and accolades for her accomplishments. She was NC Mother of the Year in 1986 and NC Handicap Worker of the Year in 1965 with Governor Dan K. Moore presiding. A Resolution by the City of Bessemer City in Memory of Lois Sexton Smith was proclaimed on December 12, 1994. And the list goes on.

Mama lived life to the fullest, with an infectious enthusiasm that touched all who met her. I can remember in college bringing friends home for the first time and gasping... "Y'all I forgot to tell you….my mom's in a wheelchair." Silence from the car. But when they arrived at our home, they simply forgot the chair as we had for all those years. I honestly think Mama forgot about it, too. Her hope, and now mine, is that her story will help anyone suffering a debilitating setback, whether it be mental or physical, find inspiration and courage.

Like Mama, make the most of life. Look for and find the joy. Make the most of what comes your way and take it in stride. Enjoy the ride. But most of all, be sure to laugh along the way. *A lot!*

Annette Smith Stilwell
Lossie's middle child

LOSSIE'S FAMILY:
Sam Smith
Annette Smith Stilwell
Lisa Smith Donini

Sitting:
William Stilwell, Annie Stilwell holding Jackson Donini, Lois,
Joseph Donini holding Caroline Donini

Next row:
Bill Stilwell, Veronica Smith, Kristen Smith, Russelll Smith,
Annette Stilwell, Erin Stilwell, Lisa Donini

Standinng:
Sam Smith

REMEMBRANCES OF LOSSIE

Don Curtis
Founder, Curtis Media Group
Chairman and CEO

It would be easy to become bitter if an accident leaves you a paraplegic in your youth. But Lois Smith was not ready for that. Instead she became determined. She beat all the odds, day-after-day and year-after-year. She gave birth to three wonderful children. She was a wife to a husband who adored her. As the editor-in-chief, only reporter, and inspiration of the town's weekly newspaper, she gave spirit and pride to the little hometown I shared with her. Week-after-week, she wrote every word that was printed! But she did more. Lois was deeply involved in every civic endeavor, and her warm smile greeted everyone daily and gave reason for all she met to smile as well. She did not know a stranger. Remarkable is the word I would choose, but remarkable is really an understatement. Unbelievable is perhaps still inadequate. It seemed that when someone said here's something you can't do, she did it! I was pleased to know her. I was inspired by her. I was honored to call her a friend. More than just a mother, more than just an editor and reporter, she was a friend to everyone she knew. I can't wait to read the book about her life.

When she was finally called to heaven at an age no one ever expected her to reach, I know that she was greeted in heaven with the words, 'Well done. Well done indeed!"

Veronica Smith
Daughter-in-Law

Lois was the embodiment of the *Serenity Prayer* by Reinhold Niebuhr:

> *God grant me the courage to change the things I can change,*
> *The serenity to accept those I cannot change,*
> *and the wisdom to know the difference*

Diane Metcalf
High School friend of Annette's

I spent a lot of time at Annette's house during high school
and I never though of Lois as handicapped. She was full of life,
laughter, and love and that's all i saw. I remember her smile, her
absolute dedication to her family — stirring a pot on the stove,
sitting at her computer, and yes, i remember the dark room too.
She was the epitome of a wonderful, loving mother and after
we grew up I had the privilege and honor of becoming her
friend, as well.

Garland Atkins
Publisher of Lois' *Bessemer City Record*

Lois Smith was one of the most talented, most humble, most
thoughtful, most delightful . . . well I could go on — but I often
wonder what she could have been had she not had to drag that
darn wheel chair around!